English for
Marketing &
Advertising

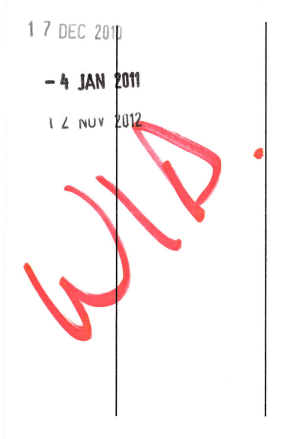

OXFORD
UNIVERSITY PRESS

OXFORD
UNIVERSITY PRESS

Great Clarendon Street, Oxford OX2 6DP

Oxford University Press is a department of the University of Oxford.
It furthers the University's objective of excellence in research, scholarship,
and education by publishing worldwide in

Oxford New York

Auckland Cape Town Dar es Salaam Hong Kong Karachi
Kuala Lumpur Madrid Melbourne Mexico City Nairobi
New Delhi Shanghai Taipei Toronto

With offices in

Argentina Austria Brazil Chile Czech Republic France Greece
Guatemala Hungary Italy Japan Poland Portugal Singapore
South Korea Switzerland Thailand Turkey Ukraine Vietnam

OXFORD and OXFORD ENGLISH are registered trade marks of
Oxford University Press in the UK and in certain other countries

First published 2007

2012 2011 2010 2009 2008
10 9 8 7 6 5 4 3

No unauthorized photocopying

ISBN: 978 0 19 457919 3

Printed in China

ACKNOWLEDGEMENTS

Prepared for OUP by: Starfish Design Editorial and Project Management Ltd

Illustrations by: Stephen May

Photo credits: istock photo library

Cover images by: Punchstock (main image/Stockbyte), Corbis (top left/
Louis Moses/zefa) and Getty Images (bottom left/Laurence Duttom/
Image Bank).

MultiROM

English for Marketing and Advertising is accompanied by a
MultiROM which has a number of features.

Interactive exercises to practise useful phrases, vocabulary,
and communication through your computer.

Listening extracts. These are in enhanced audio format that
can be played on a conventional CD-player or through the
audio player on your computer.

If you have any problems, please check the technical support
section of the readme file on the MultiROM.

Contents

About the book

In today's business world, anyone working in marketing or advertising needs English in order to do their job. Whether you are talking to clients, discussing new advertising campaigns for your company, establishing a new marketing plan, or writing a press release – you will be using English more and more.

English for Marketing and Advertising is aimed at anyone who works in marketing and advertising. The book covers all the essential responsibilities of marketing and advertising departments. There is particular emphasis on the relevant vocabulary and speaking skills needed to work efficiently in English. Telephoning, emailing, meetings, and presentations are practised, alongside the important specialist vocabulary relating to branding, market research, advertising rates, direct marketing, and public relations.

English for Marketing and Advertising consists of seven units. Each unit begins with a **Starter**, which consists of small exercises, brainstorming, or a quiz. Following this there are dialogues, texts, and authentic documents along with a variety of exercises which allow important vocabulary and expressions to be learnt in context. Realistic listenings (dialogues, presentations, lectures) on the accompanying **MultiROM** allow you to practise your listening comprehension and to improve your communication skills. Throughout the units you will be referred to the **Partner Files**, where you will have the opportunity to practise all the language of the unit in realistic role-plays.

English for Marketing and Advertising deals with important topics relating to this sector, such as finding customers, marketing strategies and tools, creating ads, and trade fairs. Every unit ends with an **Output** text, which addresses the topic of the unit and leads to discussion. Finally the book closes with a fun crossword to **Test yourself!** on all you have learnt over the previous seven units.

At the back of **English for Marketing and Advertising** you will find the **Answer key**, which you can use to check your answers. You will also find the **Partner Files**, a **Glossary** and an **A–Z word list**. This includes a column of phonetics and a space for you to write the translations of the words in your own language. You can also use the **Useful phrases and vocabulary** section if you need to look up expressions quickly whilst at work.

The **MultiROM** contains all the **Listening extracts** from the book. These can be played through the audio player on your computer, or through a conventional CD-player. In order to give yourself extra listening practice, listen to it in your car or copy to your MP3-player. The **Interactive exercises** let you review your learning by doing **Useful phrases, Vocabulary, and Communication** exercises on your computer, which will be particularly valuable if you are using the book for self-study.

1 Introduction to marketing and advertising

STARTER

Look at the following marketing and advertising activities. Can you add any?

Doing market research

Liaising with the sales department

Providing support for customer service

Drawing up a marketing plan

Showing visitors around the company

Writing press releases

Commissioning advertising

Creating advertisements

Presenting at a trade fair

Talking to customers

Speaking to journalists

Reading trade magazines

Now answer the questions.

1 Are all of these activities done in your company? If not, which ones are outsourced?
2 Which of the activities are you responsible for? Which are most important in your job?
3 Who do you speak to in English? What about? What English texts do you read? What do you write in English?
4 What is the most difficult to do in English?

1 **Look at the following extracts from job advertisements. Match the titles to the job descriptions.**

brand manager • director of marketing • head of PR • marketing assistant

1
His or her primary responsibility is to provide direct support to the media buyers. S/he will also track media mentions, support customer service, manage our relationship management tools, and provide other assistance within the marketing department when needed.

2
The successful candidate must be an excellent manager and have a proven track record in leading a large department. The mission is to develop and execute a comprehensive marketing plan that reinforces our leadership position. Direct responsibilities include media relations, PR, marketing communications, planning, and more.

3
The job involves managing all aspects of public relations, publicity, etc. The right person will have solid writing skills and strong relationships with the appropriate media outlets. The position reports directly to the CEO. The salary is based on experience.

4
You will be responsible for developing and executing brand strategies and marketing initiatives for an assigned product line to meet revenue, profitability, and budget targets. Requires strong knowledge of marketing principles and practices, and the ability to lead cross-functional teams to accomplish a successful go-to-market strategy. This position reports directly to the Director of Marketing.

2 **Match words from each column to make collocations from the job ads. Then match the collocations to the definitions (a–g).**

1	media	knowledge
2	customer	line
3	brand	mentions
4	product	relations
5	strong	responsibility
6	primary	service
7	public	strategies

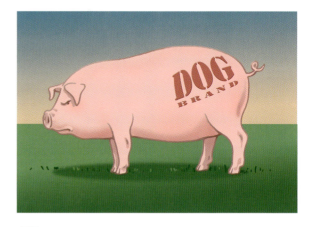

a a related series of items sold by a company (e.g. education software titles offered by a publisher)

b the department that deals directly with consumers

c communication with the general public

☐ 1 d items where the company's name is seen in newspapers, magazines, and websites

e main task or function

f good understanding

g ways of promoting a brand

3 **Here are some more jobs and companies involved in marketing and advertising. Match them to the descriptions.**

> ad agency • art director • copywriter • graphic designer • market research firm • PR officer

1 One of this person's responsibilities is to create logos.
2 This company is responsible for creating advertisements.
3 This company might conduct a survey to find out more about your customer.
4 This person supervises the design staff.
5 This person interacts with the media to communicate important company information to the public.
6 This person writes the text for advertisements.

4 **Think about your job responsibilities and write an ad for your own job (or the job you would like to have). Here are some phrases to get you started.**

> **USEFUL PHRASES**
>
> **Talking about job descriptions**
> The job involves …
> You /The successful candidate will be responsible for …
> The right person will be in charge of …
> Direct responsibilities include …

AUDIO
2

5 **Anna works in a medium-sized sporting goods company and is telling a new business partner who's who in the department. Listen to the dialogue and complete the organigram.**

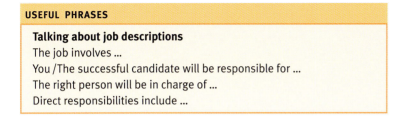

_____ ᵃ, director of marketing

_____ ᵇ, branding specialist

_____ ᶜ, public relations officer

_____ ᵈ, product manager

_____ ᵉ, public relations assistant

_____ ᶠ, product management assistant

AUDIO
2

Listen again and complete the sentences from the dialogue.

1 We have separate _____ for sales and marketing.

2 I'm the public relations _____ here.

3 I _____ directly to Sabrina, who's the _____ of marketing.

4 If you need to talk to somebody about individual _____ , then you should contact

   Vittore or his _____ , Thomas.

5 Sylvia is _____ for the image of our various brands.

6   **Now draw an organigram for your own company or department. Use the following words and phrases to describe yourself and the people you work with.**

to report to

to supervise

to answer to

to be in charge of

to be responsible for

I report to the director of sales and marketing.

AUDIO

3 – 5

7   **Representatives of three companies – a bank, a budget airline, and a car company – are giving presentations on their companies. Listen and make a note of each company's brand values.**

Company 1:   *quality*_____   _____   _____

Company 2:   _____   _____   _____

Company 3:   _____   _____   _____

Which company is the bank, which is the budget airline, and which is the car company?

AUDIO

3 – 5

8   **Listen again and complete these sentences from the presentations with words from the box.**

> associate • communicate • emphasize • external • obvious • project •
> promote • remind • reputation • widely

1   We have three main brand values which we try to _____ in all our internal and

_____ communication.

2   Our customers _____ us with the highest quality products.

3   Our products are _____ seen as the safest on the market.

4   That's something we can _____ through our brand.

5   We have always had a _____ for coming up with new products and we try to

_____ that through our brand.

6   For us, the customer always comes first and we want to constantly _____ both
ourselves and our customers of that fact.

7   That's something we continually _____ in our marketing.

8   Hopefully that is _____ from our logo and corporate design.

BILLION-DOLLAR BRANDS

There are about fifty brands in the world which generate one billion dollars' worth of sales. The category with the largest number is the beverage industry. Four tobacco brands and three snack foods are also in the list. IT, diapers, soup, detergent, telecoms, chewing gum, film, and razors also feature. Can you name any of these brands? Which are the biggest in your country?

---

9   **Look at the adjectives below and write down a company or product you associate with each one. Then compare your results with your partner. Did you write down any of the same companies/ products?**

reliable: _____

easy to use: _____

luxurious: _____

good value for money: _____

trustworthy: _____

innovative: _____

unusual: _____

user friendly: _____

Which characteristics do you want people to associate with your products or services? Why?

What are your company's brand values (or what should they be)? Does your company have a slogan? What is it?

10   **Work with a partner. First use the profiles in the Partner Files to discuss the brand values of 'your' company, the national rail service. Then present your ideas to the rest of the class.**

USEFUL PHRASES

Presenting your ideas
We think / feel that ...
In our opinion, the best options are ...
The most effective values for our company would be ...

PARTNER FILES → Partner A   File 1, p. 62
Partner B   File 8, p. 63

11   **How many expressions with *brand* do you know? Match the terms in the box with their definitions.**

brand awareness • brand equity • brand extension • brand identity • brand image • brand loyalty • brand name • branding • derived brand • off-brand

1   What a brand is called.
2   How much people are aware of a brand.
3   What a company wants people to think about a brand.
4   What people actually think about a brand.
5   When a product doesn't fit the company's brand.
6   The value (either monetary or not) that a brand adds to a product or service.
7   When people like a brand and buy it again and again.
8   When a product or service is associated with a brand.
9   When an existing brand is used to support a new range of products.
10   When a component of a product becomes a brand in its own right (e.g. Intel in PCs).

OUTPUT

Read this article from *The Marketer's Guide* and answer the questions.

Brand love *by Peter Vane*

Branding, branding, branding: If you haven't heard the word, you've been under a rock for the last, oh, ten years. But is all the talk about branding just so much hype?

In a word: no. I think that branding is the most important point your company can consider – and everyone should consider it. And those of you who sell to companies – office chairs, obscure chemicals, you know who you are – you should be paying attention too.

It's not enough just to have everyone recognize your brand name or your logo. Branding is about connecting, after all, and everyone in marketing needs to know how to make their product connect to their customer. The best brand has a rational as well as an emotional appeal, and speaks to your customer's head as well as his or her heart. You

want your brand to be something the customer knows is the best – and feels is the best too.

Today, everyone's talking about iPods, and not just as state-of-the-art musical devices. When people talk about their iPods, you might think they're talking about a best friend: 'I'd never go anywhere without it!' 'If I had to choose between my iPod and my girlfriend, well …' Despite the number of me-too products designed to compete with the iPods, the original still has the largest market share. Why? Brand loyalty.

And remember, once you've inspired brand loyalty in your customers, you can't betray them and change the story of your brand. Cadbury, for example, has a reputation for their chocolates. But when they introduced Cadbury's *soup*, it flopped. The problem was that the product was off-brand, and didn't fit with the expectations people had about Cadbury's products.

So remember that when you're telling a story about your product, the story has to be consistent. Very few products live forever. iPods might already be yesterday's news. But establish your brand, and people will remember it. When Apple introduces its next new idea, millions of people will be paying attention, ready to fall in love again.

OVER TO YOU

- How important is branding to your company? How important is it in your culture?
- Make a list of brands you like and brands you don't like. Explain your feelings. (Did you have a bad experience with the brand? Was it advertised with an amusing or a horrible commercial?)

2 Finding the customer

Tricia works for a small sporting goods store in Manchester. Look at what she says about her typical customer.

Our typical customer is health-conscious and enjoys keeping fit, but doesn't play sport professionally. He or she is more interested in sport as a hobby. Our customer is more concerned with good value for money than with having cutting-edge fashions and designs.

Who is your typical customer? Write a profile of this person. How is this information reflected in your marketing strategy? What are some of the ways you learn more about your customers and their needs?

1 Use the words in the box to complete the following list of ways to learn about your customers.

clients • competitors • find out • listening • loyal customers •
new trends • sales records • search terms

1 Email *loyal customers* directly with one or two questions.

2 Examine the _____ that people type into your website's search function. Which items are people looking for?

3 Schedule a social event, such as a wine tasting, for existing or potential _____ , and use this as an opportunity to _____ more about what they want.

4 Compare your marketing approach with that of your _____ . What areas are they targeting that you aren't?

5 Read trade journals to learn about _____ . This will help you stay ahead of the competition.

6 Study your _____ to see what facts you already have about the people who buy from you.

7 Spend time in a shop or at a trade fair _____ to people. What do they talk about? What questions do they ask?

Now work together with a partner to decide which methods are best for researching:

a a new product or service
b an existing product or service.

AUDIO
6

2 The marketing team at Euphony, a telecoms company, wants to research the market for mobile phones made specifically for children. Listen to the following discussion between three members of the team and make a note of the six data collection methods they mention.

Data collection methods

1 *postal survey*

2 _____

3 _____

4 _____

5 _____

6 _____

What advantages and disadvantages do the different methods have? Which is the cheapest? Which is the most expensive? Listen again if necessary.

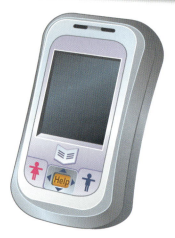

DID YOU KNOW?

Market research terms vary between Britain and the US. For example, an *individual interview* in Britain is often called a *one-on-one* or an *in-person survey* in the US, a *street interview* is called a *sidewalk survey*, and a *postal survey* is called a *mail survey*.

AUDIO
6

3 Listen to the dialogue again (or look at the transcript on page 69) and find words to fit the following definitions.

1 useful answer: _____

2 a survey group which is not typical of a target group: _____

3 model of a product in development: _____

4 percentage of people who complete a survey: _____

5 the group of people a company wants to sell to: _____

6 information known about a customer: _____

Now complete the sentences below using the correct form of the words you have found.

a   Rolex's _____ is wealthy people who see a watch as a status symbol.

b   When you log on to a website, the pages you look at and the amount of time you spend on them are saved in your _____ .

c   Even the best-designed surveys only have a _____ of about 4%, so don't set your expectations too high.

d   A _____ will make the data you gather worthless, so think carefully about who fills in your questionnaires.

e   We did an online survey but we didn't get many _____ . Most of the visitors to our website aren't customers.

f   Once the product development department has created a _____ , we can display it at trade fairs. I'm sure it will attract more people to our stand.

4 **Look at these other methods for assessing available information and collecting new information about your customers. Sort them into the correct category. Can you add any more to the table?**

desk / field research

purchasing information

feedback forms

email surveys

opinion polls

panel surveys

pre-testing

sales statistics

Sources of available data	Collection of new data
sales statistics	opinion polls

Have you ever used any of these methods or the ones mentioned in the dialogue in exercise 2? Which gave the best results? Why?

5   Look at the following scenarios. Work with a partner to decide which data collection method is best for each one. Try to use phrases from the Useful Phrases box below to give your opinions and to agree or disagree.

1

From online to on the beach

An online travel agency wants to know how satisfied its customers are with its services.

2

Mmm – fruit to fizz!

A beverage company wants to test three new soft drinks.

3

A local transportation company wants to gather demographic information on its current passengers.

4

WORKING HARD FOR YOU – because you worked hard for it

A financial consulting firm for very wealthy people wants to introduce a new wealth management package.

USEFUL PHRASES

Giving your opinion
I think / feel that …
It would be great to …
We definitely should …

Asking others for their opinion
What do you think, [Mark]?
[Harry], do you agree?
[Wendy], would you like to say a few words
  about that?

Agreeing
Me too.
Me neither. / Neither do I.
That's true.
Good point.

Disagreeing
I don't think …
Sure, but …
I see what you mean, but …

6   Heike, one of the members of Euphony's marketing team, is calling Greg at Inside the Market, a market research firm in the UK. Listen to the conversation and complete Greg's notes.

Heike – Euphony
• needs survey for _____ 1
• _____ 2 survey is best
• _____ 3 target group
• qualitative and _____ 4 data:
  – price and _____ 5 the phone should have
  – number of people interested, what willing to pay
• basic demographic information:
  – _____ 6 and _____ 7
• call Heike back on _____ 8

AUDIO
7

Now complete this extract from the conversation. Then listen again and check your answers.

Greg   Any _____¹ details? Should we ask about their _____²
and values towards children, for instance?

Heike   That would be interesting information, of course but to be honest, we don't want
to _____³ the _____⁴. If it's too long people will just get
_____⁵.

7 **The marketing research firm has prepared the following script for the telephone survey.
Work in pairs to ask and answer the questions.**

Inside the Market

Project number: 185083

Internal Title: Euphony Mobile for Children Survey

Hello, my name is [*name*], and I'd like to ask you a few questions about mobile
phones for children. Do you have a few minutes?

[*if caller agrees*]
Great, thank you. So, I'm calling on behalf of a company which wants to make a
mobile phone specifically for children.

1 **Could I ask you how much you would pay for the phone?**

☐ £40   ☐ £80   ☐ £120   ☐ £160

2 **How important are the following features to you?**

	very important	important	not very important	unimportant
a colourful design				
a headset				
light-weight				
long battery life				
built-in tracking				
being able to pre-programme numbers				

3 **What other features are important to you?**

_____

4 **How interested would you be in buying such a product?**

☐ very interested   ☐ interested   ☐ not very interested   ☐ not interested

---

**Do you think this is a good survey? Why or why not? Are there any questions you would add
or change?**

8 **The questions below were taken from a survey. Use the words in brackets (and the correct tense) to complete them.**

1   How many calls _____ (you / make) per day with your mobile phone?

☐ 1–3 a day   ☐ 3–5 a day   ☐ 6+ a day

2   When _____ (you / buy) your phone?

☐ less than 2 years ago   ☐ 2–3 years ago   ☐ more than 3 years ago

3   What _____ (convince) you to buy the phone you currently have?

☐ price   ☐ features   ☐ other _____

4   Why _____ (you / want) to buy a new phone now?

☐ old one doesn't work   ☐ want more features

☐ want the latest model   ☐ other (please specify) _____

5   _____ (you / ever / buy) a mobile phone for someone else?

☐ yes   ☐ no

6   _____ (anyone / ever / give) you a mobile phone as a gift?

☐ yes   ☐ no

Now ask your partner the questions and note his / her answers. How could a mobile phone manufacturer use this information?

> **USEFUL PHRASES**
>
> **Asking questions**
> Could I ask you how much you would pay for the phone?
> How important are the following features to you?
> What other features are important to you?
> How often would you ...?
> Can you tell me more about that?
> When did you last ...?
> Have you ever used / purchased a ...?
> What would you like / be willing to ...?

9 **Work with a partner to decide on a market research plan for 'your' company, a budget airline. Use the profiles in the Partner Files to decide on methods and to brainstorm survey questions.**

PARTNER FILES   Partner A   File 2, p. 62
Partner B   File 11, p. 63

10 Greg has presented the following summary of results. Read it through and match the headings from the box to the sections.

Appendices • Major findings • Purpose • Secondary findings

Inside the Market

187 Piccadilly • London W1J 9LE • United Kingdom
Telephone: +44 (0)20 7439 9920 • Fax: +44 (0)20 7494 1310
Email: greg.whelk@insidethemarket.co.uk

Executive summary

_____ 1

To decide what the demand is for a child-specific mobile phone, to see what features are important to the target market, and to gauge interest in the product.

_____ 2

It is very important to restrict the numbers that can be dialled and to include a headset. A tracking system is somewhat important. Potential customers are willing to pay up to 100 GBP for such a product. Respondents with children or with close relatives who have children are very interested in buying such a product. Parents are very concerned about the possible health dangers of children using mobile phones.

_____ 3

Design and size are unimportant, but the product should be durable.

_____ 4

1) Demographics
2) Tabulated survey information
3) Selected comments

Now decide whether the statements below are true or false. Correct the false statements.

a One goal of the survey was to see how interested people are in a mobile phone for children.
b Parents want their children to be able to dial any number.
c People without children are also interested in buying mobile phones for children.
d Parents think that mobile phones might be harmful to children.
e Respondents said they want the phone to be small and last a long time without breaking.

OUTPUT

Read these comments about market research and say which opinion(s) you agree with.

> *Every company should examine their product line carefully at least once a year. The best way to do this is with market research. And, ideally, people in the company should be involved in the research process. Otherwise, you risk becoming out of touch with your target market. My boss, Alison, is always saying 'I don't think customers would want that.' When did she last speak to one of our customers?*

> *When I think of market research, I think of that old saying: 'Begin with the end in mind.' If you want clear results you can use, you have to tell your market research firm exactly what you want. Don't let them be creative or make their own suggestions. Remember: you're the one in charge.*

> *Market research? I'm sorry, but I think it's a complete waste of time. I know exactly what my customers need already. The challenge isn't giving them what they want, but giving it to them at the **price** that they want.*

> *I think that most companies spend too much time speaking to their customers about what they want, and not enough time looking at their competitors. It's not just competitors in their own field. Everyone in your focus group might agree that you make the best chocolate bar in the business, but that doesn't help you sell your products if no one wants to eat chocolate!*

OVER TO YOU

- How do you analyse your competitors?
- Do you think market research is worth doing in your company (or industry)? Why or why not?
- What are the advantages of doing your own market research versus outsourcing it?

3 Planning a marketing strategy

Which of the following points do you discuss when drawing up a marketing plan? Are there any factors you can add?

marketing activities (past and present) ☐

current position ☐

sales projections and costs ☐

results from last year ☐

analysis of competitors ☐

objectives ☐

marketing tactics ☐

problems and opportunities ☐

benchmarking ☐

marketing strategy ☐

implementation ☐

situation analysis (target market, competitors, economic climate) ☐

AUDIO
8

1 Martin is the marketing manager of a telecommunications company. He is telling his colleagues about the marketing mix for a new product. Listen and take notes on the four Ps.

- Product   *have everything you need to connect to the*

   Internet,

   _____

- Price   _____

- Placement   _____

   _____

- Promotion   _____

   _____

TELUNITE

Now listen again and complete the phrases from the presentation.

1   The _____ of our cable package are that you get …

2   We will be _____ customers through ads on …

3   Our product will then be immediately _____ to customers in …

4   We will _____ that customers will have …

5   We haven't _____ a price yet …

6   Because our product is in the _____ phase, our _____ model should …

2   **Which words in the box are used to talk about which P? Sort them into the correct category.**

> advertising • appearance • channels of distribution •
> discount • financing • list price • location • logistics •
> media • public relations • quality • service

Product _____
_____
_____
_____
_____

Price _____
_____
_____
_____

Placement _____
_____
_____
_____
_____

Promotion _____
_____
_____
_____

Can you add any more words to the categories?

DID YOU KNOW?

When people talk about the marketing mix, they often refer to the four Ps: product, price, placement, and promotion. Some people use the term *place* instead of *placement*; both terms are just another way to refer to distribution. Some people also talk about seven Ps and include *people* or *participants*, *processes* (takes service into account), and *physical evidence* (the appearance of your business).

3   **Use the following chart to make notes on the four Ps of one of your company's products or services. Then use your notes to give a short presentation of the product or service to the class.**

Product What are the important aspects of your product? Why do people want to buy your product?	
Price What factors affect your price?	
Placement When and where is your product available to customers?	
Promotion List the ways in which you reach customers. What are your contact points?	

4   **Martin is organizing a meeting to discuss the prices for the cable Internet package. Put the following sentences in the correct order to complete the email.**

a   Could you have a look and let me know if there's anything you'd like to add or change?
b   As you probably know, we need to think about scheduling a meeting to discuss our pricing strategy for our new cable Internet package.
c   Hope you all had a nice weekend.
d   Please let me know if you can attend by the end of the day.
e   How about next Tuesday at 9 a.m.?
f   I'm also attaching an outline of what I'd like to talk about.

Delete   Reply   Reply All   Forward   Print

Hi team,

_____ 1
_____ 2
_____ 3
_____ 4
_____ 5
_____ 6

Thanks for your help.

Regards,
Martin

USEFUL PHRASES

Writing emails

Remember that not all emails are informal. Business emails to people outside the company tend to be like letters; they follow certain conventions (see below) and are written with punctuation and capital letters. Errors can give a bad impression, so be sure to check your spelling using an online dictionary or the spellcheck function of your email program.

Greetings and closes

Dear Ms Flores – Yours sincerely *(very formal)*
Hello Geoff – Best wishes *(neutral)*
Hi Martin – All the best *(less formal)*

Pleasantries

Hope all's well with you.
Hope you (all) had a nice weekend.
How was your weekend?

Closes for saying thank you

Many thanks.
Thanks for your help.
Cheers *(informal & British)*

Tip

Remember to capitalize the first letter in an email (or letter):

Dear Mr Steinblatt
Thank you for your message …

---

5 **Look at three replies to Martin's email. Use the words in the box to complete the them.**

> attachment • attend • best • cheers • hope • input • mind • postpone • see

Hi

Just wanted to let you know that I can _____ [1] the meeting. I've looked at your outline and can't think of anything to add. _____ [2] you on Tuesday.

Hello Martin

I'm still at the conference in Darmstadt and won't be back in town until Wednesday. Would it be possible to _____ [3] the meeting? I'm back in the office on Thursday and free all day. If not, I'll send you my ideas by email. By the way, I couldn't open the _____ [4]. Could you send it again in a different format?

_____ [5]

Hi Martin

Tuesday morning is fine for me. I noticed that you didn't send your message to Laura. Would you _____ [6] if I invited her to join us? It might be useful to have her _____ [7]. I'll have a look at the attachment and will get in touch if there's anything missing.

_____ [8] you had a nice weekend too.

All the _____ [9]

Graham

6   **Now read the attachment that Martin sent to his team and find words or phrases that mean the following:**

1   when a customer pays the same fee each month / year / etc.
2   to sell a group of things (like products or services) as a package
3   reduced price
4   another word for *product launch*
5   enhanced features or services that customers have to pay more money for

Cable Internet package pricing model

I have a few questions I'd like everyone to think about in advance of the meeting. As you know, we're introducing a new DSL package, and we need to decide what we should be charging for our services. Some points to consider are:

- What should our pricing model be? A monthly flat fee or charge by data volume?
- Do we want to offer different prices in different regions?
- Should we bundle our services and offer a discount?
- What about adopting a penetration pricing strategy for the roll-out? How long should these prices be valid for (3 months, 6 months, …)?
- What optional extras shall we offer (e.g. guaranteed 24-hour servicing)?

Please think about these questions, and we can discuss everything in more detail

7   **Match these different pricing models to the definitions.**

1   captive product pricing
2   economy pricing
3   geographical pricing
4   penetration pricing
5   premium pricing
6   price skimming

a   pricing goods/services as cheaply as possible
b   charging a high price for an item where you have a competitive advantage
c   charging a high price for a unique high-quality item
d   pricing goods at a very low price to encourage people to buy them – often the prices are later raised
e   pricing according to area where goods are sold
f   pricing one item very low and its complement very high

Now decide which model is being discussed.

A   Naturally we need to price our goods lower in countries with a lower per-capita income.

B   We at Chamonix Écrit believe the quality of our pens justifies their cost.

C   These low prices will only be in effect for the first six months. After that they will be raised by 10–25%.

D   Yes, the printers we sell are inexpensive, but we charge quite a bit for the ink cartridges.

E   Our own-label brands sugar, flour, and milk have much lower prices than the brand-name competitors.

8 **Martin and two members of his team are meeting to discuss pricing. Use the profiles in the Partner Files to take part in the meeting. Try to use the phrases on page 14 for giving your opinion and for agreeing or disagreeing.**

PARTNER FILES ➤ Partner A   File 3, p. 62
Partner B   File 9, p. 63
Partner C   File 10, p. 63

9 **Look at these terms used to talk about pricing. Can you add three more?**

recommended retail price · break-even point · profit margin · **price** · going rate · price war · overheads

Now use the words to complete the sentences below.

'Looking at the competition, €25/month seems to be the _____ [1]. It's what most people are charging.'

'We can sell the modems for €100 each. They only cost €20 in total to produce and distribute, so we would have a healthy _____ [2] of €80.'

'€59.99 is a good _____

_____ [3]. We can suggest that stores sell it for that much, but if they want to use it as a loss leader and sell it for less, then that's fine too.'

'What I'm afraid of is an all-out _____ _____ [4], when our company and the competition are all fighting for the same customers. We don't want to cut our prices so low that we go out of business.'

'We need to establish our _____ [5]. When does the amount we're earning cover our costs?'

'Luckily, we have low _____ [6]. Our rent is very low, and we got a great deal on our office equipment.'

TELUNITE

FULL BROADBAND PACKAGE

Get connected for

€25.00

per month

10 Other than price, what factors are important for your product differentiation? Think about a product you know and discuss it in terms of these factors.

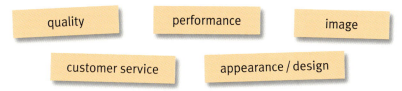

quality

performance

image

customer service

appearance / design

AUDIO

9

11 Martin is giving a presentation to management about the positioning strategy he has developed with his team. Listen and answer the questions below.

1 What is the company's target market?
2 Why is their product superior to other packages?
3 How can they prove that their product is the best?

AUDIO

9

Listen again and complete the phrases from the presentation.

1 We are _____ customers who are …
2 Extensive testing _____ that we provide …
3 Speed of access is _____ why our product is better.
4 Another reason is that we _____ every new customer with a free …

12 Now write a positioning strategy for your company. Include the following points.

1 your target customer
2 what you do for your customer and how you do it
3 how you are better than your competitors

> **USEFUL PHRASES**
>
> Our customers are …
> The main benefits our product offers are …
> We provide a superior product by …

OUTPUT **Read the following article from marketing guru Cheryl Hattiaghandi's website and answer the questions below.**

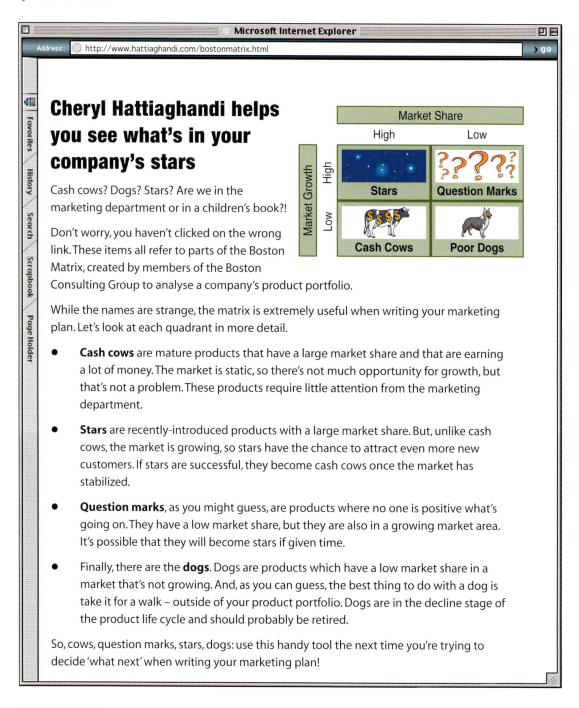

Cheryl Hattiaghandi helps you see what's in your company's stars

Cash cows? Dogs? Stars? Are we in the marketing department or in a children's book?!

Don't worry, you haven't clicked on the wrong link. These items all refer to parts of the Boston Matrix, created by members of the Boston Consulting Group to analyse a company's product portfolio.

While the names are strange, the matrix is extremely useful when writing your marketing plan. Let's look at each quadrant in more detail.

- **Cash cows** are mature products that have a large market share and that are earning a lot of money. The market is static, so there's not much opportunity for growth, but that's not a problem. These products require little attention from the marketing department.

- **Stars** are recently-introduced products with a large market share. But, unlike cash cows, the market is growing, so stars have the chance to attract even more new customers. If stars are successful, they become cash cows once the market has stabilized.

- **Question marks**, as you might guess, are products where no one is positive what's going on. They have a low market share, but they are also in a growing market area. It's possible that they will become stars if given time.

- Finally, there are the **dogs**. Dogs are products which have a low market share in a market that's not growing. And, as you can guess, the best thing to do with a dog is take it for a walk – outside of your product portfolio. Dogs are in the decline stage of the product life cycle and should probably be retired.

So, cows, question marks, stars, dogs: use this handy tool the next time you're trying to decide 'what next' when writing your marketing plan!

OVER TO YOU

- How useful do you think the Boston Matrix is?
- Can you think of a potential star product or service in your industry that your company doesn't make or offer?

4 Creating ads

STARTER

Look at the advertisement below and analyse it according to the AIDA model. Does it:

catch the audience's **A**ttention,
make them **I**nterested,
create **D**esire,
and state the **A**ction the audience should take (e.g. *Call now!*)?

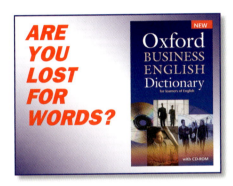

Do you agree with this model for advertising? Why or why not? Think of a few ads you've seen or heard lately and use the AIDA model to analyse them.

1 Look at the steps involved in organizing an advertising campaign and put them in the correct order.

- a analyse impact
- b approve design
- c choose the media
- d commission ad agency
- e define target group
- f determine the desired response
- g establish message
- h place ads

Can you add any other steps? Which steps are you or your company responsible for?

> **DID YOU KNOW?**
>
> The word *advertisement* is pronounced differently in the UK and the USA; in the UK the stress is on the second syllable [əd'vɜːtɪsmənt] whereas in the USA it is on the third syllable [ˌædvər'taɪzmənt]. The short form for advertisement is *ad* (also *advert* in the UK).

Where do you see a lot of advertising?

What commercials do you like?

What can you not advertise on TV in your country?

When is it very expensive to advertise?

AUDIO
10

2   **Joys of Germany is an organization in charge of promoting tourism in Germany. One of their staff is in London to meet Red Arrow, an advertising agency. Listen and find out why they want to advertise.**

☐ to introduce a new product

☐ to promote a special price

☐ to create or maintain awareness for a product

☐ to remarket a product

Now answer the questions below.

1   According to Joys of Germany, what sort of image does Germany have abroad?
2   What do they say are the stereotypes associated with Germany?
3   What kind of visitors does Joys of Germany want to attract to Germany?
4   Why is it important to design advertising which is specific to a certain country?

3   **Complete these sentences from the dialogue with the words from the box. Listen again if necessary.**

achieve • appeal • appeal • campaign • create • looking • outside • perspective

1   Tell me what you're _____ for.

2   But that's why it's important for us to _____ a new image.

3   We think that someone from _____ will have a fresh _____ …

4   We want to make sure our ads _____ to people in the UK.

5   I understand what you're trying to _____ .

6   You need an insider to design an ad _____ with the maximum _____ .

4 **Look at what some people have said when discussing their ad campaigns. Match the highlighted words or phrases (1–6) with their synonyms (a–f).**

a   change perceptions
b   generate a buzz
c   have an emotional appeal

d   have a rational appeal
e   rebrand
f   reinforce the existing image

White Noise's portable music players aren't popular because they're the cheapest or even the most technologically advanced products out there. Rather, they're popular because, quite simply, people love them. The new ad campaign should attract people based on how they feel [1].

We want to get people talking about our product [2].

Choritos are currently thought of as a high-fat snack. We need to reinvent [3] *our product as healthy and convenient.*

The ads should transform people's ideas [4] *about Germany.*

The advertisements should make a logical argument [5]. *Viewers should buy our toothpaste because it's scientifically proven to be the best in the industry.*

Our minivans already dominate the market, and they're still in the growth stage of their life cycle. So the ads should simply emphasize what people already think [6]: *that they're both safe and fun to drive.*

5 **You are in charge of commissioning a new ad campaign to promote Soyatastic, a new soya-based drink. Use the notes and the phrases below to explain to an ad agency what you want.**

Soyatastic
- *doing well in organic grocery stores*
- *people at conventional grocery stores think drink is boring, plain*
  → *introducing four new flavours (raspberry, blood orange, mango, blueberry)*
- *most important → taste*
- *also → healthy, large sizes are good value for money*

USEFUL PHRASES

Discussing an ad campaign
Typically, our products have appealed to …
We have a high market share among teenagers / 18–25-year-old men.
We want to appeal to a younger / older audience.
Our [*name of product*] is very well known, but we want to raise the profile of our …
It's important for us to reinforce our brand's positive image / to change perceptions of our product.
We'd like to rebrand our product / to change our image / to create a new image.

6   **How do you think advertisements vary between countries? Read the opinions below. Do any of them surprise you?**

A   *I can tell the difference between a German ad and a British one immediately. I find German advertising very direct, whereas British advertising tends to be much more subtle. You know, a British ad for a chocolate bar might be all about something that has nothing to do with chocolate, but which somehow manages to evoke the idea of self-indulgence: a woman in a bath, for example. A German ad for a chocolate bar will always have a chocolate bar in it.*

B   *Henry Ford said that a car can be any colour as long as it's black, and I feel the same way about advertising. A really good ad campaign will work across cultures and appeal to basic human needs – the only thing you need to change is the language.*

C   *I was in Japan a few years ago and was shocked to see how many famous Hollywood stars were advertising everyday products like cars and bath soap. They'd never do ads like that in the US because it would harm their reputation here. I'm not sure why it's OK to do it in Asia, though. But a friend from Kyoto visited me recently, and she mentioned that these days, Japanese companies prefer to use Japanese actors in their ads. Apparently the West is losing its appeal!*

D   *Sure, something like fancy French perfume can be marketed in a similar way around the world: the only thing that changes is how sexy the ad is allowed to be! But the ad campaigns for our wines are completely different in, say, the US and France. Our American ads show a couple drinking wine in a very exclusive restaurant; it's clearly a special occasion. And our French ads show a group of adults, obviously old friends, having a casual meal at home. The product is the same, but the 'packaging' is completely different.*

Which opinion refers to:

1   universal advertising?

2   a change in status of foreign stars?

3   differences in advertising styles?

4   a product that has a different status in different cultures?

Think about the industry you work in. How important is it to adapt advertising for different cultures? What differences in advertising have you noticed when travelling abroad?

AUDIO

11

7 Two colleagues at Red Arrow are discussing which advertising channels they should use in the Joys of Germany ad campaign. Listen to the dialogue and make a list of the channels they mention in the table below. Then add one more item to each category.

Print media	Online	Outdoor	Other
magazines			

8 Match the two parts of the phrases to make collocations from the dialogue.

1	eye-catching		an issue to something
2	to devote		channels
3	good		exposure
4	to make		images
5	print		media
6	repeat		opportunity
7	traditional		sense

Now use the correct form of the collocations above to complete the sentences.

1 Our area newspaper often _____ to presenting local businesses, and many of

the shopowners see this as a _____ to advertise.

2 _____ is essential for getting your message across to customers. If they only see your advertisement once, they won't remember it.

3 We operate on a very tight budget, so for us it doesn't _____ to advertise on

_____ such as radio or television. We focus on online marketing instead.

4 What I like most about our new ad campaign are the _____.
No one could forget that picture of the penguin and the dog!

5 One of the disadvantages of advertisements in _____ is sometimes your advert gets 'lost', for example when there are several of them on the same page.

9   Tracy and Justin, two colleagues at Red Arrow, meet to decide how to spend the advertising budget for Joys of Germany. First look at the information below. Then take the role of Tracy (Partner A) or Justin (Partner B) and use your notes in the Partner Files to discuss the various opinions. Choose two options for the campaign.

PARTNER FILES →   Partner A   File 4, p. 62
Partner B   File 16, p. 64

Budget €50,000

Ad in large general magazines: €6,000 per issue

Ad in small specialist magazines: €2,000 per issue

Buying keywords: €100–1,000 per word

Two-week bus ads in major British cities: €500 per city

Postcards: €1,000 for 50,000 postcards + €1,000 distribution costs

10   As part of the campaign, Tracy and Justin have come up with this print ad. How effective do you think it is? Do you think it will appeal to the target audience? What does it say about Germany?

11 **Joys of Germany received the ad from Red Arrow. One of their consultants is now writing back to request a few changes. Complete the email with words from the box.**

actually • all in all • also • as • how about • however • just • otherwise

From: carsten@joys-of-germany.de   To: tracy@redarrow.com

Dear Tracy,

Thank you very much for the ad. We are very happy with the simple design,

_____ [1] we think we can use the grid format in many different types of

ads. The look is interesting without being too unconventional.

_____ [2], we're a little concerned about the photograph on the right.

It is _____ [3] not a great view of the TV tower and we would rather

emphasize another, undiscovered feature of the country. _____ [4] a

photograph of a fashion designer at work instead? _____ [5], we like your

inclusion of the cathedral, but the image is quite dark. It would be nice to find

something a little brighter, I don't think that should be difficult.

_____ [6], though, we're very happy with what you've done!

_____ [7] give me a call if you'd like to discuss the images in more detail.

_____ [8], I look forward to hearing from you soon.

Regards,
Carsten

USEFUL PHRASES

Giving feedback
When giving feedback, try to use the sandwich approach. Begin and end your email or conversation with positive feedback (the *bread*), and put any criticism in the middle (the *filling*). That way you begin and end on a positive note, and it is more likely that the person you are criticizing will still feel confident and motivated.

Positive feedback
We're very happy with what you've done.
We really like …

Criticism
We think that the colours are not bright
  enough. /too bright.
We think that the images might be too …

Remember to soften criticism by using words such as
  a little, quite and *rather.*
We're a little concerned about …
… but the image is quite dark.

Finally, be specific about what changes you want.
… it would be nice to find something a little brighter.
How about … instead?

12 Use phrases from page 33 to give feedback on ads in this unit or on any ads you have seen recently in magazines or newspapers. Try to use the sandwich approach.

13 Tracy also recommended advertising via the internet and sent Carsten the link to the following article. Read the article and answer the questions below.

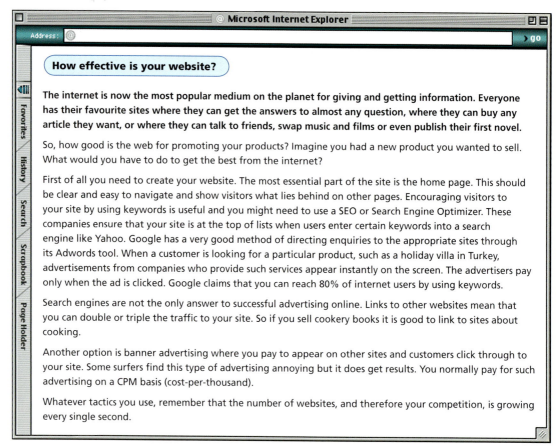

> @ Microsoft Internet Explorer
>
> Address: @
>
> ### How effective is your website?
>
> The internet is now the most popular medium on the planet for giving and getting information. Everyone has their favourite sites where they can get the answers to almost any question, where they can buy any article they want, or where they can talk to friends, swap music and films or even publish their first novel.
>
> So, how good is the web for promoting your products? Imagine you had a new product you wanted to sell. What would you have to do to get the best from the internet?
>
> First of all you need to create your website. The most essential part of the site is the home page. This should be clear and easy to navigate and show visitors what lies behind on other pages. Encouraging visitors to your site by using keywords is useful and you might need to use a SEO or Search Engine Optimizer. These companies ensure that your site is at the top of lists when users enter certain keywords into a search engine like Yahoo. Google has a very good method of directing enquiries to the appropriate sites through its Adwords tool. When a customer is looking for a particular product, such as a holiday villa in Turkey, advertisements from companies who provide such services appear instantly on the screen. The advertisers pay only when the ad is clicked. Google claims that you can reach 80% of internet users by using keywords.
>
> Search engines are not the only answer to successful advertising online. Links to other websites mean that you can double or triple the traffic to your site. So if you sell cookery books it is good to link to sites about cooking.
>
> Another option is banner advertising where you pay to appear on other sites and customers click through to your site. Some surfers find this type of advertising annoying but it does get results. You normally pay for such advertising on a CPM basis (cost-per-thousand).
>
> Whatever tactics you use, remember that the number of websites, and therefore your competition, is growing every single second.

(Favorites History Search Scrapbook Page Holder)

According to the article what are the advantages of using keywords?

How effective do you think this form of advertising is?

14 Carsten and a colleague have brainstormed the following list of keywords to buy for Joys of Germany.

holiday in Europe
dynamic
Germany
clubbing
cycling
fashion
nightlife

Do you agree? Are there any words you would add or delete?

Now think about a product or service you are advertising. Which keywords would you choose to promote it?

15 **Carsten has written to the British trade magazine *Travel Today* about placing advertisements. First unscramble the words to form sentences, then put the sentences in the correct order.**

Dear Mr Sykes,

☐ a I would be / hot / dedicated to / any issues / travel destinations / especially / interested in /

☐ b and I look forward / you soon / Thank you / to / for your help, / hearing from

☐ c the circulation / to know / Specifically, I / of your magazine / would like

☐ d send me / to the email address / rate sheet / could you please / an advertising / And finally, / below?

1 e I am writing / in your / on advertising / to request / publication *Travel Today* / information

☐ f please / your advertising schedule / Also, / send me / could you / for next year?

Yours sincerely,
Carsten Kleinöd

Joys of Germany   carsten@joys-of-germany.de
Schönhauser Allee 171
80437 München
Germany

16 **Look at the rate sheet and find the following information:**

a What is the discount for a full year?
b How much is a full-page colour ad?
c What costs 1,500 euros?
d What is the cheapest ad you can place?

Advertising rate sheet — Effective January 2008

COLOUR RATES (€)
Inside front cover 6,000
Inside back cover 5,000
Inside front cover gatefold 13,000
First double page spread 9,000
Second double page spread 8,000
Double page spread 7,000
Full page 4,000
Half page 2,000
Eighth page 800
Sixteenth page 400

SPOT COLOUR RATES
Full page 3,500
Half page 1,800
Quarter page 1,000
Eighth page 750
Sixteenth page 400

MONO RATES
Full page 4,000
Half page 1,500
Quarter page 850

AD SIZES

Size	Type Area mm	Trim mm	Bleed mm
DPS	257 x 388	273 x 412	283 x 422
Page	257 x 185	273 x 206	283 x 216
1/2 V	257 x 91		
1/2 H	127 x 185		
1/4 R	127 x 91		
1/4 V	257 x 44		
1/4 H	62 x 185		
1/8 V	127 x 44		
1/8 H	62 x 91		
1/16	62 x 44		

Gatefold on application

A digital proof is required for all colour advertisements.

DISCOUNTS
52 consecutive insertions 20%
26 consecutive insertions 15%

Read this article from a marketing trade publication about choosing an ad agency and discuss the questions that follow.

Creating the ad that will work for you
by Sara O'Toole

Do any of these scenarios sound familiar?

- Annette Torrefazioni was very excited when she first met Colin Durell of Stone & Slade. 'Colin was extremely professional, and had worked with a number of luxury food sellers,' Torrefazioni explained. 'His portfolio of ads exactly matched the image our company wanted. But once I'd signed the contract, I was shocked to learn that Colin wouldn't be handling my account. Instead, a junior staff member just out of art school would be designing my ad. When the first proofs came, I was really disappointed. It just wasn't what I had in mind.'

- 'We were really impressed with their client list,' says Thorsten Sauer, marketing manager at Durchfahrt GmbH. 'They were working with some of the top names in the industry. I didn't realize this would mean that our small account would be at the bottom of their priority list. I realized afterwards that we should have gone with a company that specialized in dealing with small firms.'

- Henri La Fontaine told of his experience with Zzzzip, a medium-sized advertising agency based in London: 'A friend of a friend told me about Zzzzip. Craig was quite professional and friendly, and we signed a contract immediately. However, a few days later I found out that our biggest competitor was working with Zzzzip too! Craig didn't see the problem, but I really wasn't comfortable with the situation. Luckily, he let me dissolve the contract.'

To avoid mishaps like the ones above, it's best to interview prospective agencies carefully. Here are our top seven tips for questions to ask.

1 *Do you handle accounts our size? What is your experience working with small/medium-sized/large companies?*

2 *Do you have an area of expertise? What is it?*

3 *Can you give me a list of current and former clients to talk to?*

4 *What is your fee structure?*

5 *Who will be handling the actual project?*

6 *Who worked on the ads in your portfolio? Are those people still with the company?*

7 *Are you working with one of our competitors?*

- Have you ever had a particularly good (or bad) experience with an ad agency? What went right (or wrong)?
- Do you agree or disagree with the tips above? Which are most difficult to put into practice? Why?
- Are there any other suggestions you can add?

5 Marketing tools

Can you add any distribution channels below? Which channels does your company use? Why?

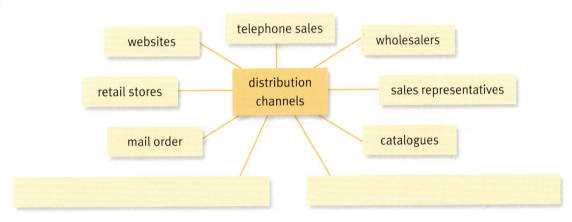

1 **Look at this website listing for a range of kitchenware. Is this a good way for the manufacturer to promote and sell its goods?**

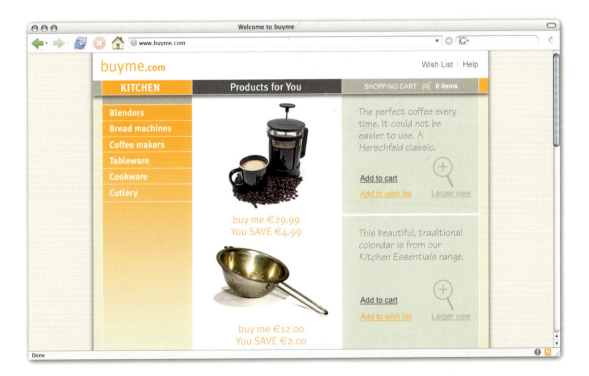

AUDIO

12

2 **Stefanie from the manufacturer Herschfeld calls her contact at *buyme.com* to complain about low sales. Listen to their conversation and decide whether the statements below are true or false. Correct the false statements.**

1 Sales of Herschfeld's goods on *buyme.com* have been lower than expected.
2 Herschfeld did not offer *buyme.com* a trade discount.
3 Herschfeld's real-world retailers are upset because *buyme.com* offers lower prices than they do.
4 Stefanie wants *buyme.com* to include two images of all the Herschfeld products they sell.
5 She also wants them to remove the prices from Herschfeld's products online.
6 The changes will be on the site later today.

Now complete the crossword with words from the dialogue.

Across

2 a product that is being highlighted for a short amount of time, e.g. on a website: *a ... product*
4 image of a product: *a product ...*
5 the price advertised for a particular product: *... price*
6 to agree something, like a price or terms, through discussion: *to ...*
7 estimates of how much a company thinks it will sell (of a product): *sales ...*
8 to not reach a goal: *to be below ...*

Down

1 a three-word expression used to describe a traditional business, i.e. one that doesn't only exist online
3 the place where you put items you want to buy: *shopping ...*

3 **Stefanie mentions a trade discount in her phone call. What other discounts are there? Match the discounts below to their definitions.**

1 ☐ trade discount
2 ☐ bulk discount
3 ☐ promotional discount
4 ☐ cash discount
5 ☐ professional discount
6 ☐ employee discount
7 ☐ seasonal discount

a a discount given to buyers purchasing a large amount
b a discount for payment in cash
c a reduced price offered on goods sold at the 'wrong' time of the year, such as ski equipment in the summer
d a discount given to people in a particular field, for example when doctors pay a reduced price for medicine
e a discount for staff
f a fixed percentage offered to a distributor
g a lower retail price for a special sale

Are all of these discounts offered in your country? What discounts does your company offer? How do they help your company reach its goals?

4   **Match the types of shop in the box with the definitions (a–h).**

chain stores • convenience stores • franchises • high-street shops • hypermarkets • mail-order stores • online stores • outlet stores

a   large no-frills stores located outside the town centre *outlet stores*_____

b   stores selling thorough the Internet _____

c   independently-owned shops licensed to trade under the same name _____

d   shops located in the centre of town _____

e   shops run by a single company with multiple locations around the country _____

f   very large stores that sells groceries, clothes, and many other products _____

g   stores selling through a catalogue posted to customers_____

h   small, independently-owned stores selling essential products_____

AUDIO

13–17

Now listen to different retailers talking about their business. Which types of 'shops' above do they mention?

Speaker 1   *high-street shops*_____   _____

Speaker 2   _____   _____

Speaker 3   _____   _____

Speaker 4   _____   _____

Speaker 5   _____   _____

5   **How much do you know about retailers in the UK and the USA? Work with a partner to describe the following shops. (If necessary, go to their websites for information.) Can you name similar retailers in your country?**

1 Marks & Spencer   (http://www.marksandspencer.com)
2 7-Eleven   (http://www.7-eleven.com)
3 Next   (http://www.next.co.uk)
4 Taco Bell   (http://www.tacobell.com)
5 Argos   (http://www.argos.co.uk)

6 **Look at this extract from Total Telemarketing's web page and match the headings to the paragraphs.**

Continual assessment

Test for success

Painstaking planning

Know your contacts

Welcome to buyme

www.buyme.com

Total Telemarketing

What We Offer

Who We Are
What We Offer
What You Get
Our Process
Our Clients
Contact Us
Home

TTM

19 St Helen's Road
York YO1 6WR
UK
T: 01534 888800
F: 01534 888801

1 _____
At Total Telemarketing, we start the process with what we call a 'discovery' phase. We build a clear picture of your business objectives and your market. We then use the information we have collected to plan your telemarketing strategy. And we make sure that both sides have clear expectations about the strategy.

2 _____
Once we have planned the approach, we test it with a 'pilot' project. This is to check if the strategy will function for you and for your market. We make sure that our plans integrate seamlessly with your marketing efforts.

3 _____
As part of your telemarketing strategy, we develop and maintain a comprehensive database of contacts and potential clients. This makes sure you have a continuous flow of good quality sales leads.

4 _____
The performance of the strategy is regularly reviewed to make sure we are delivering what you need. Written reports keep you up to date with the success of the approach.

Done

AUDIO

18

Deborah Waters, a partner at Total Telemarketing, is giving a presentation on her company. Listen and match her comments with the sections of the web page above.

Comment a _____

Comment b _____

Comment c _____

Comment d _____

7 Complete the table with the missing verbs and nouns. Check the web page and transcript in exercise 6 if you need help.

Verb	Noun
to assess	1
2	delivery
3	development
to discover	4
to expect	5
6	maintenance
to perform	7
to succeed	8

8 Deborah Waters has just received the following email from Geldsburg, a Swiss manufacturer of hand-held barcode scanners. Geldsburg are expanding their services in the UK and are interested in hiring Total Telemarketing to design a campaign for them. Use the words in the box to complete the email.

appreciate • developed • interested • priced • reach • require • visited • would like

Dear Ms Waters,

I have just _____ 1 your website, and am _____ 2 in learning more about the services you offer. Specifically, I _____ 3 to know the cost of your services. Are they _____ 4 per call or per hour? Also, how much preparation time do you _____ 5 before you're ready to begin? And finally, how much support do you need from us once the campaign has been _____ 6?

I would _____ 7 the opportunity to discuss these questions further. You can _____ 8 me at +41 80 3858 1905.

Yours sincerely,

Volker Harding
Marketing Assistant

9 **Work with a partner. Use the profiles in the Partner Files and the phrases below to role-play a telephone conversation between Volker (Partner A) and Deborah (Partner B).**

> **USEFUL PHRASES**
>
> **Telephoning – getting through**
> Hello, [company]. [Name] speaking.
> Hello, this is [name] from [company]. I'd like to speak to [name], please.
> Just a moment. I'll put you through.
> Speaking. What can I do for you?

PARTNER FILES Partner A   File 6, p. 63
Partner B   File 14, p. 64

10 **The Geldsburg marketing team have also decided to do a direct mailing for the scanner and have commissioned Direct Sales, a British direct marketing firm, to draw up a letter. Read the letter and summarize the benefits of the hand-held scanners.**

■**GELDSBURG**■
Heimplatz 101, 8001 Zurich

Dear Ms Christie

We are writing to introduce a faster and more effective way to let your customers pay for their purchases. Our new hand-held barcode scanners allow your customers to pay for their purchases where they are, without having to find a till.

Our scanners will connect remotely to verify credit or debit card payment. Customers can sign for their purchases on the scanner itself. And the scanners come with a handy adjustable belt, so your shop assistants can easily carry them at all times. The easy-to-read display is visible in all lighting conditions.

The machine automatically prints out a 'paid' sticker with the name of the product and the date, to ensure that only products which have been paid for are taken from the store. This is a feature that no other scanner on the market offers.

To learn more about the scanners, view our web presentation on our website (www.geldsburg.com) or call us on 0800 583 9910.

We look forward to doing business with you!

Best wishes
Your Geldsburg Team

Benefits:

11 Below are some tips on direct marketing. Work with a partner to rank the tips from most (1) to least (7) important. Which of these tips does the letter in exercise 10 follow?

- [ ] a Emphasize what makes you different from the competition (such as price, delivery services, after-service sales).
- [ ] b Use words that sell, such as *new* and *free*. (Trial periods and money-back guarantees can encourage customers to try a new product.)
- [ ] c Use white space. (Keep the letter to the point and use short paragraphs and bulleted or numbered lists to make points. Make it easy for the reader to get through the whole letter.)
- [ ] d Put yourself in your customers' shoes. (Focus on benefits, not product features, and build rapport by saying *you* and *your*.)
- [ ] e Use product endorsements (quotes from satisfied customers).
- [ ] f Call to action! Tell the reader what to do, e.g. *Call now to ... .*
- [ ] g Restate your USP in your P.S. (Response rate testing indicates that the typical reader's eye moves down the page to the P.S. before he or she reads the rest of the letter!)

12 The Geldsburg marketing team has called Direct Sales with some feedback on the letter. Use these notes and the tips above to write a second draft. (Or write a first draft of your own direct marketing letter.) Try to use phrases from the Useful Phrases box below.

Telephone call

From: Geldsburg
To:
About: Feedback on letter
Date: Time:

1) Highlight bulk discount offered to retailers ordering 20 or more scanners

2) Emphasize security features for the credit card check

3) Include a customer quote (two below, more available):
Jennifer Tierny, Floor Manager, Shopsave: 'I can't believe how easy it is to operate. The options are right in front of you.'

Chris Creswell, Senior Manager, Handy DIY, says, 'Geldsburg's scanners have all the features we need and are also simple to use. We definitely made the right decision.'

USEFUL PHRASES

Writing to the customer (direct mailing)
We are writing to introduce/tell you about/announce (a new product).
To learn more about (our product), visit *www.geldsburg.com* or call us on 0800 583 9910.
When you receive your trial model, you'll quickly see the benefits of (our product).
If you contact us before 10 March, you'll receive a free sample.
We look forward to hearing from you soon!

OUTPUT

What's the best marketing idea you've ever seen? This question was the subject of a recent poll conducted by a marketing trade publication. Look at some answers given by marketing and advertising professionals below.

John Webster, *Marketing Manager*

The best marketing idea I've ever seen? That would have to be a butcher's shop in my town. They sent sausages in the form of flower bouquets to all the local catering firms! I'm not sure how much new business they got, but everyone had a good laugh.

Vicky Chen, *Creative Director*

I was impressed by a rock band who put MP3 files with the title of their new single on all the major music exchange websites. When the fans downloaded the file, they heard an advertisement for the band's new record instead of the single. They found this so funny that they began emailing the single to friends, and album sales skyrocketed.

Veronica Weiss, *Marketing Assistant*

If you buy ten books or more in a year at Claridge's Books, you'll be sent a free book on your birthday. It certainly encourages me to buy from *them* instead of from one of the larger chain stores or online bookshops.

Craig Lukasiewicz, *Director of Online Marketing*

One thing I've noticed recently is advertising products in blogs. The blog will look like a website created and maintained by an individual, but in fact, it's created by a company. I suspect this will become more popular in the next few years. But whether this is ethical or not is another question.

OVER TO YOU

- What are some of the more unusual or clever marketing efforts that you've heard of?
- How effective do you think these types of marketing campaigns are?
- Do you know of any unsuccessful marketing campaigns? Why did they go wrong? How could they have been improved?

6 Presenting your public face

Company newsletters, home pages, press releases, sponsoring, and press conferences are all ways to promote your company. Find an example of each below.

1
Vadi Vision is proud to announce that it will be sponsoring a new campaign to promote eye health awareness.

2
You'll be pleased to hear that in the last year, Vadi Vision has pulled ahead of its main competitor to win the market share in optical sales.

3
When Mr Vadi started Vadi Vision 21 years ago, he had no idea of what a success it would be.

4
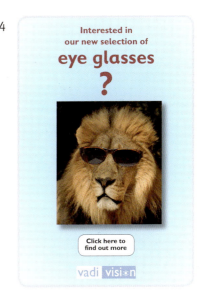
Interested in our new selection of
eye glasses
?
Click here to find out more
vadi vision

Which of the above items are you responsible for writing (in your own language or English)? What other methods (other than advertising) do you use to promote your company?

AUDIO
19

1 A marketing consultant is giving a presentation called *How to make your website into an effective marketing tool*. First look at the features below. Do you think it's a good or bad idea for websites to have them? Now listen to the presentation. Does the consultant agree with you?

	good idea	bad idea		good idea	bad idea
easy navigation	☐	☐	large images	☐	☐
site map	☐	☐	'look inside' option	☐	☐
search function	☐	☐	simple shopping interface	☐	☐
Flash introduction	☐	☐	complicated language	☐	☐
pop-up windows	☐	☐			

Now answer these questions. Listen again if necessary.

1   What is the maximum number of times visitors should have to click to find the information they want?
2   According to surveys, what do visitors do with Flash introductions?
3   Which company made the 'look inside' option popular?
4   What are two examples of the 'look inside' option?
5   Who should check the content on your website if you are writing in a foreign language?

2   **Use the information from the presentation (you can find the transcript on pages 71–72) and your own ideas to make a checklist of dos and don'ts. Then use this checklist to examine the strengths and weaknesses of your own (or another) company's home page.**

Dos	Don'ts

3   **What makes a website easy to navigate? Look at the two home pages on the next page and answer the questions.**

1   Where do you click to ...
    a   get help with a product?
    b   see the company's products?
    c   get a mailing address?
    d   find out about the company's history?
    e   read articles about the company?
2   Where can you search for a word or phrase?

Which home page do you think is more attractive to customers? Why? What do you think customers expect from a website?

4   **How is your Internet English? Solve the anagrams and find them in the puzzle.**

1   oalwddno
2   swen
3   tobua su (5, 2)
4   nicolato
5   tcntneo
6   egaim
7   charse ignene (6, 6)

e	c	m	a	c	u	g	e	w	j	t	d	e
d	o	w	n	l	o	a	d	b	e	n	h	g
g	n	i	g	o	m	u	t	d	w	e	l	k
t	t	w	r	c	z	u	f	r	t	w	o	p
k	e	s	s	a	b	o	u	t	u	s	z	u
z	n	i	e	t	e	t	u	j	g	d	f	h
r	t	p	z	i	m	a	g	e	a	u	f	k
j	g	e	u	o	y	t	r	d	t	k	i	n
a	d	g	r	n	e	w	v	r	j	k	n	e
s	e	a	r	c	h	e	n	g	i	n	e	l

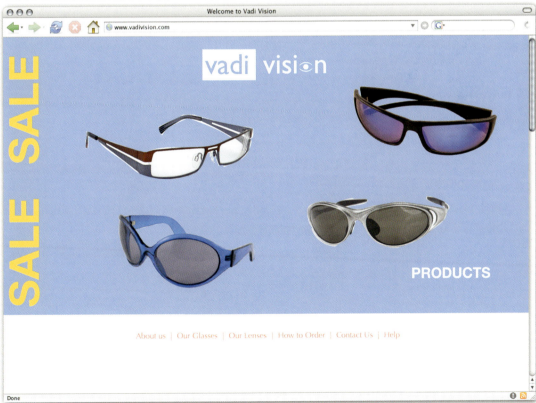

5   **Claudia Felber works for the marketing department of Vadi Vision, a Swiss lens manufacturer. In order to raise her company's profile in the UK, she has been asked to choose a charity to sponsor. First read these excerpts from letters sent to her company.**

1

We at the London-based Sleet Street Gallery would like to offer you the opportunity to sponsor the framing of our photographs for our forthcoming exhibition. In exchange for your help, we will include your logo on all promotional materials and within the gallery itself. We believe that an exhibition showcasing modern views of the city is an ideal way for a company manufacturing eye care products to promote itself abroad.

3

SEEING FURTHER is organizing donations of old eye glasses to be made to low-income communities in Central Asia. This will be a high-profile campaign in which several celebrities will be participating, and is sure to receive extensive media coverage. To be included in our sponsor list, we are asking for a donation of £ 1,000.

2

You surely realize the importance of regular check-ups to ensure healthy eyes, but unfortunately many people in Britain don't. I am therefore requesting a donation towards developing a public campaign. 'Eyes on the Eyes' will bring travelling eye examination vans to communities around the UK. The logos of the sponsoring companies will be featured on all vans.

Now work with a partner to role-play a discussion between Claudia (Partner A) and her colleague (Partner B) about which company to sponsor.

PARTNER FILES   Partner A   File 7, p. 63
Partner B   File 15, p. 64

DID YOU KNOW?

Charity is a term that refers to donating money, goods, or time to people in need. Particularly in the US, companies are often judged by their social actions as well as their financial success, and many companies involved in charitable community efforts describe themselves as corporate citizens. The causes they choose to support generally reflect the company's target market.

Some larger companies allow employees to have paid time off to work on local community projects, or even to have 'career breaks' to do charity work.

Do you know of any companies in your country that do this?

6 **Claudia has written the following announcement for the company website. Read it and complete it with the words in the box.**

funded • help • make • participated • prevent • supporting

Vadi Vision in the News

Vadi Vision has recently _____ [1] in a venture to help people in Britain get the eye care they need. Vadi Vision has _____ [2] a travelling eye inspection van which allows people to get a check-up without having to _____ [3] an appointment. By _____ [4] *Eyes on the Eyes*, Vadi Vision shows its commitment to helping British eyes. We don't just want to _____ [5] solve eye problems: we also want to _____ [6] those problems from happening.

Eyes on the Eyes

vadi vision

7 **Claudia is preparing a press release for a new product. She calls Chris, one of Vadi Vision's good customers, to ask him for a testimonial. Listen to the telephone conversation. What quote does Chris give Claudia to use?**

Now decide whether the statements which follow are true or false. Correct the false statements.

1 Claudia found out about Chris and how much he likes Vadi Vision's lenses because he wrote her an email.
2 Chris doesn't want to say that Vadi Vision's lenses are the best because he doesn't want to make the other suppliers that he works with unhappy.
3 Many of Eye Care Central's customers have heard about Vadi Vision through their sponsorship of *Eyes on the Eyes*.
4 Vadi Vision will be giving away free samples of their lenses at a trade fair next week.

8 **Match the two parts to make sentences from the dialogue. Listen again if necessary.**

1 I'm hoping
2 I'm writing a press release
3 Our customer services rep forwarded
4 This would be a great quote
5 I was wondering
6 Thanks so much for
7 Make sure you come

a your help.
b to include.
c you can help me.
d me your email.
e by our stand.
f for our new ultra-hard lenses.
g if you would mind us using it?

Writing press releases

1 Use a headline (in bold) that summarizes what the press release is about.

2 Here are some typical ways to start a press release.
[Company] *announced today that ...*
[Company] *is proud to announce the launch of the new ...*
[Company] *is introducing ...*

3 Remember to list contact information at the top of the release, and tell the readers in the body of the press release where they can go to get details:
For more information about ..., contact ...
More information about ... can be found at www.company.com.
Businesses interested in more information on ... should contact ...

9 **Claudia has written a press release for the new lenses. Put the parts of the press release in the right order.**

a Contact: Claudia Felber, claudia.felber@vadivision.com
Telephone: + 41 20 759 29 55
Fax: + 41 20 759 29 60
www.vadivision.com

b The Diamond Line ultra-hard lens is suitable for glasses wearers with single and bifocal vision problems. And not only are the lenses ultra-hard, but they're also extra-thin. This makes them especially attractive for those glasses wearers requiring high-prescription lenses.

c Eyecare professionals interested in information and samples should contact their Vadi Vision representative or send an email inquiry to diamondline@vadivision.com.

d Vadi Vision is one of the best known and most respected eyewear companies in Europe. As Chris Baker of Eye Care Central in London testifies: 'Our customers often ask for Vadi Vision lenses by name.'

e Zürich, 12 March 20..

f Vadi Vision is pleased to announce the release of a new ultra-hard lens. This lens is more durable than any other product on the market.

g FOR IMMEDIATE RELEASE

h **Vadi Vision releases a new ultra-hard lens**

Does your company have a style guide for writing press releases in English? Work with a partner to write a press release for your own (or a fictitious) company. Try to use phrases from the box above. See also the article on page 52.

10   **Claudia has prepared a holiday letter to send out to Vadi Vision's distributors and retailers. Complete the sentences with words from the box.**

appreciate • committed • eventful • greetings • launch • partnership • successful • welcome

vadi visi⊙n

Dear [*Name goes here*],

We at Vadi Vision want to pass on our holiday _____ [1] to you.

This year has been an _____ [2] one for Vadi Vision.
We made news in Britain with our *Eyes on the Eyes* campaign to encourage eye health. The campaign has been so _____ [3] that we plan to _____ [4] similar efforts in other European countries.

We have made waves with our new Diamond Line series of lenses.
These ultra-hard lenses are becoming especially popular among athletes, who _____ [5] the lenses' durability.

This year has also seen some changes at Vadi Vision. As you know, our CEO, John Vadi, recently left the company on his well-earned retirement. We would like to _____ [6] Gilda Greenwald to our team as the new CEO.

Despite these changes, Vadi Vision remains _____ [7] to eye care. We have greatly enjoyed working together with you over the past year, and look forward to a continued _____ [8] in the coming year.

With all the very best for the New Year,

Vadi Vision

vadi visi⊙n

Now write a holiday letter to send to your company's English-speaking contacts.

Read the following article from a magazine on public relations.

Writing a killer press release

You've all seen them: the press releases that would put any reader to sleep. You've barely glanced at the title before you're ready to curl up in bed. *Campbell Associates is moving into cutting-edge new headquarters!* 'But who cares about Campbell Associates? Who *are* Campbell Associates, anyway?' you ask yourself.

It takes more than an exclamation mark to catch a reader's attention. So read on for some tips on how to write a press release that will get read – and published!

1 Keep things real.
Do not exaggerate when you write. Instead, make sure you deal with the facts. Journalists get dozens of press releases a day, and words like 'revolutionary' and 'ground-breaking' get old very quickly, especially when these words are describing very ordinary events.

2 See the story from the reporter's point of view.
Present your news as a story. The focus doesn't have to be on your company. What you want is something that people will want to read about. So focus on the people who use your products and services, and that will make your story come to life.

3 Create a headline that will grab your readers' attention.
Brainstorm four or five titles for an important press release, and then come back to them the next morning. See which one seems the most interesting to you.

4 Proofread carefully.
A badly-written press release won't get read. Get help if you need it: there are a number of good, professional PR agencies out there if you're not able to write perfect copy in English, for example.

5 Keep it short.
Ideally, give the press release to someone who doesn't know anything about the topic, and have them look at it for fifteen seconds. When they give it back to you, can they tell you the most important points? If not, you need to revise what you've written.

- What do you think of these tips? Can you think of any examples?
- What tips can you add to this list?
- Have you ever written press releases for your company? If so, what did you find easy/difficult?

7 Marketing through trade fairs

Look at these products that companies often give away to their customers and discuss the questions below with a partner.

fountain pen

USB stick

conference file

personal data assistant

umbrella

mouse mat

ballpoint pen

golf tees

conference bag

1 What do these items say about the image the company wants to project?
2 Which giveaway would you most like to receive?
3 What giveaways does your company have? Would you like to introduce any new ones?

1 **Kirstin Butler works for the marketing department of Natural Solutions, a biotech company. She has received a brochure about a trade fair that takes place in London each year. Read this excerpt from the brochure and answer the questions below.**

1   What kind of trade fair is International Biotech Europe?
2   Who might book a stand?
3   How many events are there?
4   What marketing campaign are the organizers planning?
5   Who will receive the guide before the events?
6   How much will press releases cost?

International Biotech Europe

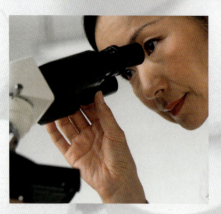

The benefits of exhibiting:
So much more than just an exhibition space

By taking part in International Biotech & Lab Automation Europe you put your company at the heart of the largest biotechnology market in Europe. And as soon as you book your exhibition stand, your company becomes part of one of the most comprehensive and high-profile marketing campaigns of the year in this sector.
Just look at all the added benefits that are included in the cost of your exhibition space:

Publicity

Your company and products will be featured in the marketing campaign to tens of thousands of professionals across the UK and Europe. The campaign will include direct mail, email and web marketing, advertising, and extensive editorial coverage in all the key magazines and journals.

Raise your profile with the press

Our experienced PR team will be promoting the event and exhibiting companies to all the key publications. You are also invited to place your press releases and company information in the International Biotech & Lab Automation Europe press office free of charge.

Promote your company online and offline

Profile your company, products, and services in the International Biotech & Lab Automation Europe guide published in both print and web format and available to your customers and prospects before, during, and after the event.

Access to additional audience from co-located event

Exhibitors at International Biotech & Lab Automation Europe will benefit from being able to promote their products and services to an additional audience from the other event. All visitors will be free to move between the two shows.

2 **Match the phrases from the brochure to the definitions.**

1 exhibition stand
2 high-profile
3 added benefits
4 editorial coverage
5 prospects
6 key publications
7 additional audience
8 co-located

a extra advantages
b in the same place
c potential customers
d the place where you show your products at a trade fair
e extra visitors
f well known
g publicity in magazine or newspaper articles
h the most important magazines and newspapers

AUDIO

21

3 **Kirstin is telling her boss, Paolo Massini, why she thinks they should attend the trade fair. Listen and answer the questions below.**

1 How well known is the event?
2 Why is Paolo not sure about the benefits of the marketing campaign?
3 In Kirstin's opinion, what is the most important benefit of the trade fair?
4 What is Paolo going to do this afternoon?
5 When is Paolo going to make a decision?

4 **Paolo has agreed that Natural Solutions should attend the trade fair and asks Kirstin to get more information. Use the notes below to write an email to Barbara Shields, the trade fair organizer.**

- discount for having stand during the whole trade fair?
- social events?
- facilities? (Internet access?)
- restaurant nearby for customer reception?
- accommodation? (no info on website)

5   One of the customer events that Natural Solutions wants to hold during the trade fair is a reception at a nearby restaurant. Kirstin asks her assistant, Michael May, to write the English version of the invitation to the event. Complete the invitation with the words in the box.

attend • introduction • join • line • place • served • walk

NATURAL SOLUTIONS

Customer reception

25 March at 1 pm

The Lemon Tree

Please select:

☐ I would like to attend

☐ I am unable to attend

Name _____

Company _____

Address _____

Phone _____

Email _____

FAX REPLY

Fax: + 39 89 280 5800

Please confirm your participation **by 4 March**.

NATURAL SOLUTIONS

To celebrate the _____ 1

of our new _____ 2 of antibiotics, we would

like to invite you to _____ 3 a reception on

Friday, 25 March at 1 pm.

The event will take _____ 4

at 'The Lemon Tree', just a short _____ 5

away from the International Biotech Europe Fair.

Refreshments will be _____ 6.

If you are able to _____ 7 us,

please let us know by fax or email.

may@natural-solutions.com

DID YOU KNOW?

During trade fairs, many companies organize social events for their customers and business partners. These events provide an excellent opportunity for business people to 'meet and greet' in an informal setting. Business is seldom discussed at such events. The focus instead is on relationship-building through small talk and introducing mutual friends. Such events are also a rare and useful chance to speak to the competition and find out more about one's rivals.

6   **Kirstin and Michael are manning the stand at the trade fair. Match their answers (a–g) with the visitors' questions and comments (1–7).**

1   Excuse me, are these memory sticks to take away?
2   Would it be possible to be put on your mailing list?
3   I'd like to discuss this with my boss first. How can I reach you?
4   Do you have some information I can take away?
5   What does your company do?
6   Do you make natural cosmetics as well?
7   I'm just browsing.

a   No, we don't. We focus on medications.
b   Yes, certainly. If you just give me your card, I'll be happy to add your name.
c   Here's my card. Feel free to call or email me.
d   They are indeed. They've got our URL printed on them, so do have a look at our website too when you get a chance. Or do you have any questions for me now?
e   Well, just let me know if you need anything.
f   We use natural sources to create effective medications.
g   Yes, let me give you one of our brochures. It lists the points we've just discussed.

AUDIO
22

Listen to the dialogues to check your answers. Then practise reading them with a partner.

7   **What are the five questions that trade fair visitors are most likely to ask you about your products or services? Write them down.**

Now exchange your questions with a partner. Take turns asking and answering questions in a trade fair situation.

USEFUL PHRASES

Attending trade fairs
Hello, may I help you?
Let me introduce myself. I'm …
Let me give you my card.
Can I ask what company you're with?
Would you like to put your name on our mailing list?
Just let me know if you need anything.

Visitors' questions
Could you tell me more about your company?
I'm interested in … . Do you offer …?
Would it be possible to be put on your mailing list?
How can I reach you?
Do you have some information I can take away?
Excuse me, are these pens/brochures to take away?

AUDIO
23

8   **Kirstin is giving a speech at the customer reception. First, read the script below and try to fill in the missing words. Then listen and check your answers.**

*Hello everyone.
I'd like to _____ ¹ you for joining us today. As you probably _____ ²,
Natural Solutions has been making great progress. Our innovative plant-based antibiotics have recently been _____ ³ for distribution. And we have a new line of cold medication that is _____ ⁴ to do very well.*

I hope you'll _____ ⁵ yourselves to the leaflets and samples at the back. Please feel _____ ⁶ to approach me if you'd like to _____ ⁷ a personal product presentation. _____ ⁸, the best solution is a natural solution, and I'm sure we have a solution for you!

9   **Work in a group of four. You are at Natural Solutions' reception. Use the phrases below and your profile in the Partner Files to socialize with the other people there.**

PARTNER FILES
Partner A   File 5, p. 62
Partner B   File 12, p. 63
Partner C   File 13, p. 64
Partner D   File 17, p. 64

USEFUL PHRASES

Socializing
Hi, I'm … – Nice to meet you.
Is this your first trip to [London/Britain/the UK]?
Where are you staying?
How are you enjoying the fair so far?
What area of [biotech] do you work in? – I'm in [sales].
I work for a company called [Natural Solutions].
Do you have a card?/Here, let me give you my card.

10   **The fair is over and Kirstin and Michael are back in the office. Kirstin has written an internal email reporting on the trade fair. First match the sentence halves below to form complete sentences. Then put the sentences in the correct order.**

1 And thanks to Gina for convincing
2 I'll be coming around to departments
3 Finally, thank you, Michael,
4 We also learned some interesting facts
5 We now have two confirmed orders,
6 Hi everyone,
   You'll be pleased to hear

a about what the competition are doing.
b as well as several promising leads.
c for all of your help in preparing for the fair.
d Hyperdrugs that our products are right for them!
e that we made lots of good contacts in London this weekend.
f to pass on the information I picked up.

OUTPUT

Look at what five marketing people say about trade fairs. Which opinion(s) do you agree with?

I think trade fairs are a complete waste of time when you factor in the cost of travel and lost working time. You usually come back feeling exhausted. And there's no way to guarantee that people will stop at your stand. Once, I went all the way to Paris, and I had only two visitors!

Something that really annoys me is when companies hire completely inexperienced people – usually pretty young women – to promote their products by handing out giveaways or whatever. Meanwhile, the marketing people who do know about the products are usually hanging out at the stand drinking cocktails and talking about anything but business! It's such a waste of time.

Some of my best contacts have come via trade fairs. You can send all the emails and brochures you want, and you can make follow-up phone calls, but there's nothing like a 30-second conversation face-to-face. It's much easier to explain the benefits of a product when you have it in your hands.

I love the buzz of a trade fair! It's not just an opportunity to sell. It's also a chance to check up on the competition and see what new ideas are out there. You can go up to a rival's stand and ask questions that they would never answer if you sent them an email. It really helps to stay in touch with the business.

The thing I hate most about trade fairs? It's the socializing. It's very easy to talk about my product and business in general, but I never know what to say when I go to receptions.

OVER TO YOU

- What do you like and dislike about trade fairs?
- Does your company attend trade fairs? Why or why not? If yes, which ones?
- What are the advantages and disadvantages of having a stand at a trade fair?
- What suggestions do you have for making the most of a trade fair visit?

Test yourself!

See how much marketing and advertising vocabulary you have learned.
Use the clues to complete the crossword puzzle.

Across

3 Another word for a TV advertisement.

8 Changing the price of a product or service depending on where it is sold: … *pricing*.

13 Information about survey respondents' age, income, education, etc: … *information*.

14 A free item, such as a pen, a mousepad, or a calendar, given to customers to promote a company.

17 A company that competes with others for the same customers: *One of Coca-Cola's main …s in the beverage market is Pepsi-Cola.*

18 The group of people that a company wants to sell its products or services to: *the … group.*

21 Comparing your company's products or services with those of the competitors: … .

24 The most important results from a market research study are called *the … … .* (5, 8)

27 To give a product or service a new image: *to … it.*

29 The stage of the product life cycle when the product's market share is increasing.

30 *A … ad* is an advertisement that appears at the top, bottom, or side of a website.

Down

1 A small group of people brought together to share their ideas and opinions for market research: *a … group.*

2 An advertisement with … *appeal* is attractive for logical reasons.

4 This person writes the text for advertisements.

5 A … … has information on a registered website user such as his or her name, password, and details of what products have been bought. (4, 7)

6 When two or more companies compete by cutting their prices it is called a *price … .*

7 A … *discount* is a discount given for very large orders, usually placed by another business.

9 Small shops with long opening hours that sell basic items such as milk, bread, cigarettes, and magazines: … *stores*.

10 The percentage of responses received to a questionnaire: *the … … .* (8, 4)

11 One of the four Ps, this refers to where the product is sold or advertised.

12 What the first word in PR stands for.

15 The average price of a product or service is called the … … . (5, 4)

16 You use a … … to show a presentation. (4, 9)

19 A positive comment about a company's product from a satisfied customer or a celebrity: *a product … .*

20 This is a two-word phrase for a series of related items sold by a single company. (7, 4)

22 To be at a trade fair stand answering visitors' questions and giving out information: *to … a stand.*

23 A … … lists the prices for advertising in a magazine or newspaper. (4, 5)

25 A … … is a fixed amount that a customer pays every month / year, etc. for a product or service. (4, 3)
The amount is not based on how often the customer uses the product or service.

26 You use it to find out what customers think.

28 Another word for the introduction in a press release.

Partner Files

UNIT 1, Exercise 10 — File 1

Partner A

You work in the marketing department of your country's national rail service. You and your partner have been asked to choose three words or phrases to serve as your organization's brand values and then to present your ideas to the board of directors. Other teams have also been asked to propose brand values and the team with the best ideas will get a promotion.

You think the brand values that represent your company are *reliability*, *comfort*, and _____ (think of your own).

Work with your partner to choose the three brand values your team wants to present. Then prepare reasons why these values are the most important.

UNIT 2, Exercise 9 — File 2

Partner A

You work for There & Back, a European budget airline. The airline currently flies between London, Paris, Rome, Berlin, Barcelona, and Amsterdam. You want to add two travel destinations in the next year, and are commissioning a market research firm to determine which of the destinations below are best:

Athens
Brussels
Lisbon
Marseilles
Sofia
Warsaw

You would prefer a focus group for your market research, but you need to discuss this with your partner first. Work together to decide on the best data collection method to use.

Then prepare a list of survey questions, and take turns to answer them (or give the survey to another pair in your class).

UNIT 3, Exercise 8 — File 3

Partner A

You are Martin/Maria and …
- prefer a pay-per-use pricing model.
- are not sure about geographical pricing. What would be the advantages of such a model?

UNIT 4, Exercise 9 — File 4

Partner A

You are Tracy. Use your notes to discuss the advertising mix and the budget with Justin.

Budget €50,000

Ad in large general magazines: €6,000 per issue *yes*

Ad in small specialist magazines: €2,000 per issue *no*

Buying keywords: *perhaps a few* €100–1,000 per word

Two-week bus ads in major British cities: €500 per city *??*

good idea
Postcards: €1,000 for 50,000 postcards + €1,000 distribution costs

UNIT 7, Exercise 9 — File 5

Partner A

First choose or fill in information to complete your profile. Then use your profile to meet people at a reception and make small talk.

Name: Erik / Erika
Title: Sales representative (choose your own country/region)
Company: Swedish Healing
Hotel:
☐ Best Western (big, noisy, good bar)
☐ Angel Arms (small, friendly, great breakfast)
☐ Mrs Long's Bed & Breakfast (quiet, outside of town – inconvenient)
☐ Ibis (big, convenient, bad food)
Home: Sweden
Company focus: Treatments for depression
Plans after conference:
☐ Go straight home, lots of work
☐ Take train to Scotland, tour the Highlands
☐ Several client meetings in London area

UNIT 5, Exercise 9	File 6

Partner A

You are Volker Harding. You have written the email on page 41 and now receive a phone call from Deborah Waters from Total Telemarketing. Note the following points:

- Long-term campaign, so you want to pay per call
- Need someone to begin asap
- Don't want to be involved at all (Total Telemarketing should handle everything)

UNIT 6, Exercise 5	File 7

Partner A

You are Claudia Felber. You have made the following notes:

Sleet Gallery – nice idea, but what kind of photos? Appropriate for corporate image? 'Eyes on the Eyes' – is it really necessary? Will it attract attention from our target market (wealthier customers)?

Seeing Further – sure to attract lots of media coverage, and helps a community with a real need

UNIT 1, Exercise 10	File 8

Partner B

You work in the marketing department of your country's national rail service. You and your partner have been asked to choose three words or phrases to serve as your organization's brand values and then to present your ideas to the board of directors. Other teams have also been asked to propose brand values and the team with the best ideas will get a promotion.

You think the brand values that represent your company are *good value for money*, *environmentally aware*, and _____ (think of your own).

Work with your partner to choose the three brand values your team wants to present. Then prepare reasons why these values are the most important.

UNIT 3, Exercise 8	File 9

Partner B

You are Carl/Carole and think it would be better to ...
- bundle services and offer a big discount in the first few months.
- use geographical pricing since your company faces more competition in some parts of the country than in others.

UNIT 3, Exercise 8	File 10

Partner C

You are Geoff/Gillian and think it would be a good idea to give away free cable modems for customers to use. Modems should only be compatible with your company's technology. (You don't want customers to switch to another company!)

UNIT 2, Exercise 9	File 11

Partner B

You work for There & Back, a European budget airline. The airline currently flies between London, Paris, Rome, Berlin, Barcelona, and Amsterdam. You want to add two travel destinations in the next year, and are commissioning a market research firm to determine which of the destinations below are best:

Athens
Brussels
Lisbon
Marseilles
Sofia
Warsaw

You would prefer a street interview for your market research, but you need to discuss this with your partner first. Work together to decide on the best data collection method to use.

Then prepare a list of survey questions, and take turns to answer them (or give the survey to another pair in your class).

UNIT 7, Exercise 9	File 12

Partner B

First choose or fill in information to complete your profile. Then use your profile to meet people at a reception and make small talk.

Name:	Michael/Michaela
Company:	Natural Solutions
Title:	Marketing assistant
Hotel:	☐ Best Western (big, noisy, good bar)
	☐ Angel Arms (small, friendly, OK breakfast)
	☐ Mrs Long's Bed & Breakfast (small, quiet, outside of town)
	☐ Ibis (big, convenient, bad food)
Home:	(your town or city: _____)
Company focus:	Natural remedies
Plans after conference:	☐ Visit friends in Cambridge
	☐ Meet with advertising agency in London
	☐ Fly to Netherlands for product presentation

UNIT 7, Exercise 9 — File 13

Partner C
First choose or fill in information to complete your profile. Then use your profile to meet people at a reception and make small talk.

Name: Bob/Barbara
Title: _____
Company: Sweevel Pharmaceuticals
Hotel:
- [ ] Best Western (big, noisy, horrible bar)
- [ ] Angel Arms (small, very rude, horrible breakfast)
- [ ] Mrs Long's Bed & Breakfast (small, quiet, no Internet access)
- [ ] Ibis (big, convenient, bad food)

Home: New York, USA
Company focus: Plant-based medical treatments
Plans after conference:
- [ ] Meet with plant-based medication firms in Great Britain
- [ ] Holiday in Cornwall – beautiful this time of year
- [ ] Return to States – daughter is getting married

UNIT 5, Exercise 9 — File 14

Partner B
You are Deborah Waters, a partner at Total Telemarketing. You are calling Volker Harding at Geldsburg to follow up on his email (on page 41). Note the following points:
Prices
Week or less: charged per call
Longer: charged per hour
Ready to begin
Depends on needs
Support
Company should be involved → better results

UNIT 6, Exercise 5 — File 15

Partner B
You are Christian/e Thielemann. You have made the following notes:

Sleet Gallery – great idea, and if the art is controversial, will attract more attention! target market: rich people, and rich people like art!
'Eyes on the Eyes' – could be interesting, and vans will get lots of attention
Seeing Further – media coverage will only last for a week or so (when campaign is launched). And we want to reach people in Britain, not Central Asia!

UNIT 4, Exercise 9 — File 16

Partner B
You are Justin. Use your notes to discuss the advertising mix and the budget with Tracy.

Budget €50,000

Ad in large general magazines: €6,000 per issue *no*

Ad in small specialist magazines: €2,000 per issue *good idea*

Buying keywords: €100–1,000 per word *need a lot to reach target audience*

Two-week bus ads in major British cities: €500 per city *No, hard to control quality*

Postcards: €1,000 for 50,000 postcards + €1,000 distribution costs *??*

UNIT 7, Exercise 9 — File 17

Partner D
First choose or fill in information to complete your profile. Then use your profile to meet people at a reception and make small talk.

Name: William/Willa
Title: Buyer
Company: Mancurian Solutions
Hotel:
- [ ] Best Western (big, fantastic)
- [ ] Angel Arms (small, too British, delicious breakfast)
- [ ] Mrs Long's Bed & Breakfast (small, inconvenient, no Internet access)
- [ ] Ibis (very noisy, convenient, good food)

Home: Oxford, England
Company focus: Antibiotics
Plans after conference:
- [ ] Train home – giving important presentation on Monday
- [ ] Visit antibiotic manufacturers in southern England
- [ ] Spend few days with sister – she lives in London

Answer key

page 6

1
1 marketing assistant
2 director of marketing
3 head of PR
4 brand manager

2 2b customer service
3g brand strategies
4a product line
5f strong knowledge
6e primary responsibility
7c public relations

page 7

3
1 graphic designer
2 ad agency
3 market research firm
4 art director
5 PR officer
6 copywriter

5
a Sabrina
b Sylvia
c Anna
d Vittore
e Uwe
f Thomas

1 departments
2 officer
3 report, director
4 products, assistant
5 responsible

page 8

7 *Company 1* (car company)
quality
safety
environmental care

Company 2 (bank)
trust
innovation
customer focus

Company 3 (budget airline)
great value for money
fun
honesty

8
1 project, external
2 associate
3 widely
4 promote
5 reputation, emphasize
6 remind
7 communicate
8 obvious

page 9

11
1 brand name
2 brand awareness
3 brand identity
4 brand image
5 off-brand
6 brand equity
7 brand loyalty
8 branding
9 brand extension
10 derived brand

page 11

1
2 search terms
3 clients, find out
4 competitors
5 new trends
6 sales records
7 listening

page 12

2
2 online survey
3 individual interviews
4 focus group
5 street interview
6 telephone survey

Sample answers
Method: postal survey
Advantages: cheap
Disadvantages:
– not very effective
– most people discard these surveys without answering

– those who answer usually skip half the questions

Method: online survey
Advantages: free
Disadvantages:
– not appropriate for this company's target group as customers tend not to buy from the website
– could lead to a skewed sample

Method: individual interviews (focus groups or street interviews)
Advantages:
– allow people to examine a prototype, leading to more informed responses
– usually have a better response rate
Disadvantages: very expensive

Method: telephone survey
Advantages:
– not as expensive as individual interviews
– allows the company to focus on its target market based on user profiles
Disadvantages: none

An online survey is the cheapest option. Doing individual interviews (focus groups or street interviews) is the most expensive option.

3
1 relevant response
2 skewed sample
3 prototype
4 response rate
5 target market/group
6 user profile

a target market/group
b user profile
c response rate
d skewed sample
e relevant responses
f prototype

page 13

4 (suggested answers)

sources of data
feedback forms
purchasing information

data collection
panel surveys
desk/field research
email surveys
pre-testing

page 14

5
1 online survey
2 street interviews
3 individual interviews
4 focus group

6
1 mobile phones for children
2 telephone
3 British
4 quantitative
5 features
6 income
7 eduction
8 Friday

page 15

1 psychographic
2 attitudes
3 overload
4 survey
5 frustrated

page 16

8
1 do you make
2 did you buy
3 convinced
4 do you want
5 Have you ever bought
6 Has anyone ever given

page 17

10 1 Purpose
2 Major findings
3 Secondary findings
4 Appendices

a True
b False: They want the phone numbers to be restricted.
c True
d True
e True and false: They want the phone to be durable but the size is not important.

UNIT 3

page 19

1 *Product:* fastest connection available, free webspace and webpage design program, virus scanner.
Price: not yet decided
Placement: cities across Europe, available within 48 hours
Promotion: ads on websites and in magazines

1 key factors
2 reaching
3 available
4 guarantee
5 fixed
6 introduction, pricing

page 20

2 *Product:* appearance, quality, service
Price: discount, financing, list price
Placement: channels of distribution, location, logistics
Promotion: advertising, media, public relations

page 21

4 1 c 2 b 3 e 4 d 5 f 6 a

page 22

5 1 attend   4 attachment   7 input
2 See   5 Cheers   8 Hope
3 postpone   6 mind   9 best

page 23

6 1 flat fee   4 roll-out
2 to bundle   5 optional extras
3 discount

7 1 f 2 a 3 e 4 d 5 c 6 b

A geographical pricing
B premium pricing
C penetration pricing
D captive product pricing
E economy pricing

page 24

9 Possible answers: loss leader, discounted price, trade price, net price

1 going rate
2 profit margin
3 recommended retail price
4 price war
5 break-even point
6 overheads

page 25

11 1 early adopters of new technology, people who want high-speed Internet access
2 It provides the fastest connection in the business.
3 by extensive testing

1 targeting
2 shows
3 the main reason
4 provide

UNIT 4

page 27

1 suggested answer
e – g – f – d – c – b – h – a

page 28

They are advertising in order to give Germany a new image as a tourist destination and to attract new tourists (to remarket a product).

2 1 Boring and traditional.
2 Sausages, the Black Forest, great composers, Oktoberfest, white wines.
3 British people who are not aware of the other side of Germany.
4 Every country has its own advertising culture and advertising norms are different in each country.

3 1 looking   4 appeal
2 create   5 achieve
3 outside, perspective 6 campaign, appeal

page 29

4 1 c 2 b 3 e 4 a 5 d 6 f

page 30

6 1 B 2 C 3 A 4 D

page 31

7 (suggested answers in brackets)
Print media: magazines, newspapers
Online: banner ads (pop-ups, pop-behinds (or pop-unders))
Outdoor: bus ads (ads on trains and other public transport, billboards, or hoardings)
Other: TV ads (radio ads), postcards (brochures, flyers, posters)

8 2 to devote an issue to something
3 good opportunity
4 to make sense
5 print media
6 repeat exposure
7 traditional channels

1 devotes an issue, good opportunity
2 Repeat exposure
3 make sense, traditional channels
4 eye-catching images
5 print media

page 33

11 1 as   5 Also
2 However   6 All in all
3 actually   7 Just
4 How about   8 Otherwise

page 34

13 (suggested answer)
Advantages: You reach 80% of Internet users. You only pay for the ad when someone clicks on it. The people you reach are interested in the products or services you offer.

page 35

15 1e I am writing to request information on advertising in your publication *Travel Today*.
2c Specifically, I would like to know the circulation of your magazine.
3f Also, could you please send me your advertising schedule for next year?
4a I would be especially interested in any issues dedicated to hot travel destinations.
5d And finally, could you please send me an advertising rate sheet to the email address below?
6b Thank you for your help, and I look forward to hearing from you soon.

16 a 20% b €4,000 c Half-page black and white
d 1/16 page

UNIT 5

page 37

STARTER
(Suggested answer)
Other channels are trade fairs, promotions, or TV shops (or shopping channels).

page 38

2 1 True
2 False: Herschfeld offered *buyme.com* a large trade discount.
3 True
4 True
5 False: She wants them to hide the prices until the products are placed in the shopping cart.
6 False: The changes will be on the site by the end of the week.

Crossword

Across	Down
2 featured	1 bricks-and-mortar
4 shot	3 cart
5 listed	
6 negotiate	
7 projections	
8 target	

3 1 f   2 a   3 g   4 b   5 d   6 e   7 c

page 39

4 b online stores   f hypermarkets
c franchises   g mail-order stores
d high-street shops h convenience stores
e chain stores

1 outlet stores
2 convenience stores; chain stores
3 convenience stores; hypermarkets
4 franchises
5 mail-order stores; online stores

5 1 Marks & Spencer is a high-street chain store that sells all sorts of items, from clothing to food.
2 7-Eleven is an American convenience store.
3 Next is a high-street shop and a chain which sells clothing.
4 Taco Bell is a franchised chain which serves Mexican fast food.
5 Argos is a British mail-order company which also sells its products online.

page 40

6 1 Painstaking planning   a 2
2 Test for success   b 4
3 Know your contacts   c 1
4 Continual assessment   d 3

page 41

7 1 assessment   5 expectation
2 to deliver   6 to maintain
3 to develop   7 performance
4 discovery   8 success

8 1 visited   5 require
2 interested   6 developed
3 would like   7 appreciate
4 priced   8 reach

page 42

10 (suggested answer)
Benefits include the following: customers don't need to find a till to pay; scanner processes payment remotely; customers can sign for their purchases on the scanner itself; the scanner is easy to carry and the display is easy to read; a 'paid' sticker shows that the product has been paid for.

page 43

11 The letter follows tips a, d, and f.

UNIT 6

page 45

STARTER
1 press release, sponsoring
2 press conference
3 company newsletter
4 home page

1 easy navigation   good
site map   good
search function   good
Flash introduction   bad
pop-up windows   bad
large images   bad
'look inside' option   good
simple shopping interface good
complicated language   bad

page 46

1 Three.
2 They skip them.
3 Amazon.
4 Product photographs from several angles; a detailed breakdown of your consulting services.
5 A native speaker.

2 *Dos:* Include a good site map and search function.
Make it clear and easy to navigate.
Keep images small.
Include a 'look-inside' option.
Include buying information.

Don'ts: Don't make your visitors click more than three times to get to where they want.
Don't include a Flash introduction or pop-up windows.
Don't use too complicated language.

3 1 a Websites 1 and 2: Click on 'help'.
   b Website 1: Use the pulldown menu next to 'products'.
      Website 2: Click on 'products'.
   c Websites 1 and 2: Click on 'contact us'.
   d Websites 1 and 2: Click on 'about us'.
   e Websites 1 and 2: Click on 'about us'.

2 Website 1: Use the field next to 'search'.

4 1 download   5 content
   2 news   6 image
   3 about us   7 search engine
   4 location

page 49

6 1 participated   4 supporting
   2 funded   5 help
   3 make   6 prevent

7 'Our customers often ask for Vadi Vision lenses by name.'
   1 False: He wrote an email to the rep, who sent the email on to Claudia.
   2 True
   3 False: The customers have heard about Vadi Vision through their advert.
   4 True

8 1 c   2 f   3 d   4 b   5 g   6 a   7 e

page 50

9 1 g   2 e   3 a   4 h   5 f   6 b   7 d   8 c

page 51

10 1 greetings   5 appreciate
    2 eventful   6 welcome
    3 successful   7 committed
    4 launch   8 partnership

UNIT 7

page 54

1 1 An international biotechnology trade fair.
   2 Pharmaceutical companies.
   3 Two.
   4 Direct mail, email, and web and coverage in all key magazines and journals.
   5 Customers and prospects.
   6 Nothing.

page 55

2 2 f   3 a   4 g   5 c   6 h   7 e   8 b

3 1 Very. Everyone in the pharmaceutical industry knows about it.
   2 Because there will be so many companies listed in the brochures.
   3 It will give them the chance to meet new prospects.
   4 He's going to look at the budget.
   5 By tomorrow.

4 (model answer)

Dear Ms Shields,

I'm writing with some questions about participating in International Biotech Europe.

First of all, could you let me know whether exhibitors receive a discount for having a stand during the entire trade fair? I would also appreciate some details on the facilities available at the venue; for example, is there wireless Internet access? Also, what social events are planned? And are there any restaurants nearby that are appropriate for a customer reception?

Finally, I couldn't locate an accommodation guide on your web page. I would be grateful if you could recommend some hotels convenient to the exhibition centre.

Thank you very much for your help. I look forward to hearing from you.

Yours sincerely,
Kirstin Butler

page 56

5 1 introduction   5 walk
   2 line   6 served
   3 attend   7 join
   4 place

page 57

6 1 d   2 b   3 c   4 g   5 f   6 a   7 e

page 58

8 1 thank   5 help
   2 know   6 free
   3 approved   7 set up
   4 expected   8 Remember

10 1 d   2 f   3 c   4 a   5 b   6 e

Order of sentences: 6 – 5 – 4 – 2 – 3 – 1

TEST YOURSELF!

pages 60–61

Across
3 commercial
8 geographical
13 demographic
14 giveaway
17 competitor
18 target
21 benchmarking
24 major findings
27 rebrand
29 growth
30 banner

Down
1 focus
2 rational
4 copywriter
5 user profile
6 war
7 bulk
9 convenience
10 response rate
11 placement
12 public
15 going rate
16 data projector
19 endorsement
20 product line
22 man
23 rate sheet
25 flat fee
26 survey
28 lead

Transcripts

UNIT 1, Exercise 5

2

Anna   Well, all marketing departments are different, aren't they?

Rob   Yes. At my company, Ben and I *are* the marketing department!

Anna   I know what you mean. I used to work for quite a small company doing all of their marketing. But the company here is a bit bigger. We have separate departments for sales and marketing. So, let me just give you some names. As you know, I'm the public relations officer here and I report directly to Sabrina, who's the director of marketing. My assistant is Uwe. You can always give him a call if you can't reach me.

Rob   Wait, Anna, let me just write this down. Sabrina and ... um, how do you spell your assistant's name?

Anna   That's U-W-E. Uwe.

Rob   Got you.

Anna   And if you need to talk to somebody about individual products, then you should contact Vittore or his assistant, Thomas.

Rob   Ah, what was that again? Vee ...?

Anna   Vittore – he's Italian. You spell that V-I-double-T-O-R-E.

Rob   OK. And Thomas. That's easy enough.

Anna   Right. Finally, Sylvia is responsible for the image of our various brands.

Rob   Great! That's very helpful.

UNIT 1, Exercise 7

3

1 We have three main brand values which we try to project in all our internal and external communication. The first is 'quality'. Our customers associate us with the highest quality products. The second is 'safety'. As you probably know, our products are widely seen as the safest on the market. And the third is 'environmental care', which is a relatively new brand value for us, but one which will become increasingly important in the future.

4

2 I'd like to tell you something about our brand values. The first, and most important, is 'trust'. In a business like ours, customers have to trust us completely, and that's something we can promote through our brand. Then we have 'innovation'. We have always had a reputation for coming up with new products, and we try to emphasize that through our brand. Another key brand value is 'customer focus'. For us, the customer always comes first and we want to constantly remind both ourselves and our customers of that fact.

5

3 Let me just move on to talk a little about our brand values. It will come as no surprise to you that our top brand value is 'great value for money'. That's something we continually communicate in our marketing. The next is 'fun'. Hopefully that is obvious from our logo and corporate design. Finally we have 'honesty'. We want customers to feel that we tell them the truth.

UNIT 2, Exercise 2

6

Corinna   Well, a postal survey would be quite cheap.

Heike   That's true, but I don't think it would be very effective.

Rupert   Neither do I. After all, every time I get one of those I usually put it straight in the bin. And the people who do answer usually skip half the questions. I think an online survey would get much better results.

Corinna   Well, it would be free, which is nice, but I don't think all our customers use our website, actually. They tend to buy our phones in shops, so I'm not sure how many relevant responses we'd get. We may end up with a skewed sample.

Heike   What about individual interviews? If we met people, we could show them a prototype and let them examine it. That way they could give a more informed response.

Rupert   Yes, and we'd also have a better response rate. So, we could either organize a focus group and invite four to six people to take part or do a street interview, and just stop people on the street and ask them questions. What do you think, Corinna?

Corinna   Well, both options have their strengths and weaknesses, but to be honest, interviews like that usually cost a fortune. I personally think that a telephone survey is the best. We can look at the user profiles we have and just call members of our target market, you know, parents with young children.

Heike   I agree completely. We should definitely focus on our target group.

Rupert   Yes, but what about the people without young children like grandparents, who buy the phone as a present for their grandchild.

Heike   Mmm, good point. It looks like we'll have to ...

UNIT 2, Exercise 6

7

Greg   Inside the Market, Greg speaking.

Heike   Hi, Greg. It's Heike from Euphony.

Greg   Oh, hello, Heike. Good to hear from you. How are things in Germany?

Heike   Not too bad. Listen, Greg, I'm calling because we'd like to do a survey for a new series of mobile phones for children and I'd like you to handle it for us.

Greg   Sounds interesting. What type of survey did you have in mind?

Heike   We decided that a telephone survey would best fit our needs.

Greg   Good. OK, let me just get a pen and we can discuss the details. OK, so, what exactly do you need to find out?

Heike   We'd like you to find out more about what our British target group expects from a phone like this.

Greg   OK, so you want to collect qualitative data?

Heike	Yes, but also quantitative: the number of people interested, what they're willing to pay, etc.
Greg	All right. What are the most important points?
Heike	Price, and what features potential customers would want the phone to have.
Greg	And what sort of demographic information should we be collecting?
Heike	Just basic information, such as income and education.
Greg	Any psychographic details? Should we ask about their attitudes and values towards children, for instance?
Heike	That would be interesting information, of course, but to be honest, we don't want to overload the survey. If it's too long people will just get frustrated. And we want to keep our respondent pool as wide as possible.
Greg	Fair enough.
Heike	So, could you tell me how long it will take to prepare the survey? And when can we expect to get the survey results?
Greg	I'll need to speak to a few colleagues here, and then get back to you. Can I give you a call on, say, Friday?
Heike	That would be great. And I'll send you an email to confirm what we've discussed.
Greg	Wonderful. So, talk to you on Friday!

UNIT 3, Exercise 1

The key factors of our cable package are that you get everything you need to connect to the Internet, and that your connection is faster than anything you can get anywhere else. You can email videos in just seconds, instead of minutes or hours. Customers also get free webspace and can use our webpage design program. And finally, our software automatically scans all incoming emails for viruses.

We will be reaching customers through ads on websites and in magazines starting in September. Our product will then be immediately available to customers in major metropolitan areas across Europe. We will guarantee that customers will have all hardware and be able to use our modems within 48 hours of placing an order.

We haven't fixed a price yet, but this will be decided in the next week or two. Because our product is in the introduction phase, our pricing model should win us as many customers as possible, as quickly as possible.

UNIT 3, Exercise 11

We are targeting customers who are early adopters of new technology and who are very interested in the advanced high-speed Internet access we provide. Extensive testing shows that we provide the fastest connection in the business due to our cutting-edge technology. Speed of access is the main reason why our product is better than our competitors'. Another reason is that we provide every new customer with a free start-up package.

UNIT 4, Exercise 2

Tracy	OK, so tell me what you're looking for.
Carsten	Well. We want to do something a bit more interesting than sausages and the Black Forest. Most of our market research shows that Germany still has a boring, traditional image abroad. As we showed during the World Cup, we have the tourist infrastructure and lots of attractions but Italy, for example, still attracts far more foreign tourists than we do.
Tracy	Maybe because of the weather?
Carsten	That's one reason, I agree. But that's why it's important for us to create a new image. We need to remind people that a holiday doesn't have to be hot to be fun.
Tracy	Interesting. Tell me more.
Carsten	Well we'd like to go beyond the stereotypes. Great composers, the Oktoberfest, white wines… . The people who are interested in these things are already coming to Germany. We need to attract new visitors who aren't yet aware of the other side of Germany.
Tracy	I see. So why do you want to work with us?
Carsten	We want to work with someone based in the UK. We think that someone from outside will have a fresh perspective and be able to rebrand us better. Every country has its advertising culture and we want to make sure our ads appeal to people in the UK.
Tracy	OK, I understand what you're trying to achieve. And if I may say so, I think that you're right. Advertising norms are different in each country, and you need an insider to design an ad campaign with the maximum appeal.

UNIT 4, Exercise 7

Tracy	As far as traditional channels go, I think they should focus on print media, especially magazines, and possibly the travel sections of some larger newspapers.
Justin	That makes sense. Magazines and newspapers often devote an issue to travel, and that would be a good opportunity to highlight Germany. What about TV ads?
Tracy	I don't think that's a good idea. Just an ad or two will use up almost the entire budget, and we can't afford the repeat exposure that a good ad campaign would need.
Justin	That's true. Banner ads, on the other hand, would make sense. People often go online to travel portals like Expedia and Hotwire without knowing where they want to travel to. They just want to go somewhere for the weekend. Seeing our ads would encourage them to check out Germany.
Tracy	Good point. And what about postcards? I can see those being very effective with a campaign like this. We could have different themes for different venues: highlight outdoor activities for postcards distributed in gyms, for example.
Justin	Yes, and postcards are popular among the 18–35 group, which Joys of Germany are targeting. We could also do bus ads in major UK cities.
Tracy	OK, so I think our task is clear. We need eye-catching images and a good slogan that we can use in a variety of places.

UNIT 5, Exercise 2

Secretary	*Buyme.com.* How can I help you?
Stefanie	Hello. Can I speak to John Bradwell, please?
Secretary	Just a moment. I'll put you through.
John	Hello?
Stefanie	Hello, John, it's Stefanie Schwarz from Herschfeld here.
John	Ah, Stefanie. Nice to hear from you. How are things?
Stefanie	Not so good, I'm afraid.
John	Oh dear.
Stefanie	That's actually why I'm calling. It's about our listings on your website. As you know, we offered *buyme.com* a large trade discount on our kitchen appliances based on the sales projections you presented.
John	Of course.
Stefanie	Well, sales in the past quarter have been well below target, as I'm sure you know. Also, our bricks-and-mortar retailers have been complaining that customers are using our listed prices on your website to negotiate a cheaper price at their shops.
John	Right.
Stefanie	So basically there are a few things I'd like you to do to deal with these problems.
John	OK.
Stefanie	First of all, I'd like you to highlight our new line of microwaves in your 'featured products' section.
John	Let me just write that down … highlight new line of microwaves in 'featured products'. OK, got you.
Stefanie	The second thing is, I'd like you to include at least two product shots of each item you list.
John	Two product shots … OK.
Stefanie	And the final thing is: could you please hide the price of the products on your main web pages?
John	What do you mean exactly?
Stefanie	Well, I've seen the feature on other shopping websites. Basically, your customers can't see the price of a particular item until they place it in their shopping cart.
John	Ah yes, I understand what you mean. Well, I'm not sure if that's possible with our system, but I'll check with the technical people and get back to you, if that's OK.
Stefanie	Right.
John	The first two things I can arrange straight away. The changes will be on the site by the end of this week.
Stefanie	That sounds good.
John	It's the least I can do. Listen, Stefanie, I'm really sorry that there have been these problems.
Stefanie	Well, let's hope these changes improve things.
John	Yes, I hope so.
Stefanie	Well, thanks for your help, John.
John	No problem. Just let me know if there's anything else I can do for you.
Stefanie	I'll do that. OK, talk to you later.
John	Bye now.

UNIT 5, Exercise 4

1 Most of our appliances have been sold at shops in the centre of town. But more and more appliances are being sold at a discount at large, no-frills stores outside the town centre.

2 To simplify the distribution process, we no longer work with small, independently-owned shops. We work mainly with stores that have multiple locations around the country. However, they always demand a deep discount, which can sometimes be a problem.

3 The candy bars we produce are sold at small shops which are open long hours, and often located in city centres or alongside petrol stations. They are also sold at very large stores that combine the features of a grocery store and a department store, and often a lot more!

4 The baked goods we manufacture are sold at stores which are independently-owned and operated, but which share the same name (which is licensed).

5 Our cameras used to be sold via catalogues sent out by post, but increasingly that outlet is dying out. Instead, our cameras are now mostly sold via the Internet.

UNIT 5, Exercise 6

a One of the things that distinguishes us from the competition is that we don't just start phoning. First we make test calls, and then we evaluate what we've done before creating a plan for the longer term.

b With telemarketing, you want to know whether your strategy is working or not. That's why we constantly check the performance of the approach. If any part of it isn't working as well as it could, we can change it.

c Some telemarketing companies speak to you for ten minutes and send you a script the next day. Not us. First we speak to your marketing team to find out as much as we can about your target market and your goals for the telemarketing campaign. Then we use this information to develop a strategy that both companies can use.

d One of the most annoying things with telemarketing agencies is lost information. Telemarketers often make no notes on the people they contact who say no. But there's a big difference between the people who say 'Never call me again' and those who say 'Well, that sounds very interesting, but we just don't have the money right now.' We keep track of those people and companies who are worth contacting again in the future.

UNIT 6, Exercise 1

So, the subject of my talk today is how to make your website into an effective marketing tool. Let me ask you: is your website something you just let the people in IT deal with? It shouldn't be. A home page is the face you show the world, so think of it as an essential marketing tool. If you don't have a clear, easy-to-navigate site, you might lose potential clients.

A good site map and search function can make it much easier for visitors to the site to find the information they need. A good rule is that they shouldn't need to click more than three times to get to where they want to go. At the same time, a lengthy Flash introduction is probably a waste of money. Surveys show that the majority of visitors simply skip these to get to the main site. The same goes for pop-up (or pop-under) windows, which nearly all web users find very irritating. And remember to keep images small so that visitors don't have to wait ten minutes for the site to download.

Your website should offer complete information on all the products and services you offer. As more and more people shop from home, visitors should be able to find out all they need to know about cost and features. A 'look inside' option, which was made popular by Amazon, is worth including: this can be anything from product photographs from several angles or a detailed breakdown of the consulting services you offer. And finally, you need either a simple shopping interface or information on how visitors can purchase your goods.

Naturally, creating a website in a foreign language can pose an extra challenge. It's important to have a native speaker check all content. However, if you're dealing with many non-native speakers, it's also essential that the content isn't too difficult to understand. If most of your customers aren't native speakers, a style which is too complicated will confuse, not impress.

UNIT 6, Exercise 7

Chris Hello, Eye Care Central, Chris speaking.
Claudia Hi Chris, this is Claudia from Vadi Vision. Chris, I'm hoping you can help me. I'm writing a press release for our new ultra-hard lenses. Our customer services rep forwarded me your email where you said that you thought our lenses were the best in the business. This would be a great quote to include, and I was wondering if you would mind us using it?
Chris Um, I'm not sure. Just between you and me, I do think Vadi Vision makes the best lenses. But we work with other suppliers too, of course, and I don't want to upset them.
Claudia I can understand that. Is there anything else positive you might be willing to say about our lenses?
Chris Well, I think a lot of our customers know about your lenses through your advertising campaign. I love the picture with the lion wearing the eye glasses! So how about something like 'Our customers often ask for Vadi Vision lenses by name'?
Claudia That sounds great! Let me just write it down ... often ask for Vadi Vision lenses by name. Thanks so much for your help, Chris.
Chris No problem, Claudia. See you at the trade fair next week?
Claudia Yes, I'll see you there! Make sure you come by our stand. We'll have some samples of our new lenses to give away.

UNIT 7, Exercise 3

Kirstin Well, it's really a very high-profile event. Everyone in the pharmaceutical industry knows about it and attends. Apart from the exposure we'll get with our stand, I think there are a lot of

added benefits, including having our name sent to companies around the world and getting an extra audience with the people attending the other trade fair. The fair will also be marketed to key publications.
Paolo Hmm. I'm not so sure. They say that they'll feature you in their marketing campaign, but that's not really accurate. There will be hundreds of companies listed in their brochures, and we'll just be one of many.
Kirstin That's true. But I do think that participating will raise our profile and make us better known. Perhaps more importantly, it will give us the chance to meet new prospects who might be interested in our company.
Paolo That's a good point. Why don't I have a look at the budget this afternoon, and give you a decision tomorrow?

UNIT 7, Exercise 6

1
Visitor 1 Excuse me, are these memory sticks to take away?
Michael They are indeed. They've got our URL printed on them, so do have a look at our website too when you get a chance. Or do you have any questions for me now?

2
Visitor 2 Would it be possible to be put on your mailing list?
Kirstin Yes, certainly. If you just give me your card, I'll be happy to add your name.

3
Visitor 3 I'd like to discuss this with my boss first. How can I reach you?
Kirstin Here's my card. Feel free to call or email me.

4
Visitor 4 Do you have some information I can take away?
Michael Yes, let me give you one of our brochures. It lists the points we've just discussed.

5
Visitor 5 What does your company do?
Kirstin We use natural sources to create effective medications.

6
Visitor 6 Do you make natural cosmetics as well?
Michael No, we don't. We focus on medications.

7
Visitor 7 I'm just browsing.
Kirstin Well, just let me know if you need anything.

UNIT 7, Exercise 8

Hello everyone. I'd like to thank you for joining us today. As you probably know, Natural Solutions has been making great progress. Our innovative plant-based antibiotics have recently been approved for distribution. And we have a new line of cold medication that is expected to do very well. I hope you'll help yourselves to the leaflets and samples at the back. Please feel free to approach me if you'd like to set up a personal product presentation. Remember, the best solution is a natural solution, and I'm sure we have a solution for you!

A–Z word list

Your translation

A
to **accompany** [əˈkʌmpəni]
to **achieve** [əˈtʃiːv]
ad agency [ˈæd eɪdʒənsi]
advertisement
   [ədˈvɜːtɪsmənt]
advertising [ˈædvətaɪzɪŋ]
advertising channel
   [ˈædvətaɪzɪŋ tʃænl]
advertising norm
   [ˈædvətaɪzɪŋ nɔːm]
amusing [əˈmjuːzɪŋ]
annoying [əˈnɔɪɪŋ]
appeal [əˈpiːl]
to **appreciate** [əˈpriːʃieɪt]
approach [əˈprəʊtʃ]
appropriate [əˈprəʊpriət]
assigned [əˈsaɪnd]
to **associate** [əˈsəʊʃieɪt]
attachment [əˈtætʃmənt]
attitude [ˈætɪtjuːd]
to **attract** [əˈtrækt]
audience [ˈɔːdiəns]
awareness [əˈweənəs]

B
baked goods [ˌbeɪkt ˈɡʊdz]
to **be under a rock**
   [ˌbi ʌndər ə ˈrɒk]
belt [belt]
benefit [ˈbenɪfɪt]
to **betray** [bɪˈtreɪ]
beverage [ˈbevərɪdʒ]
brand [brænd]
brand value [ˈbrænd væljuː]
branding [ˈbrændɪŋ]
breakdown [ˈbreɪkdaʊn]
break-even point
   [breɪk ˈiːvn pɔɪnt]
bricks-and-mortar retailer
   [brɪks ən ˈmɔːtə riːteɪlə]
brochure [ˈbrəʊʃə]
to **browse** [braʊz]
budget airline
   [ˈbʌdʒɪt eəlaɪn]
to **build rapport** [bɪld ræˈpɔː]
built-in [ˌbɪltˈɪn]
bulleted [ˈbʊlɪtɪd]
to **bundle** [ˈbʌndl]

C
to **call sb back** [ˌkɔːl ˈbæk]
campaign [kæmˈpeɪn]
cash discount [ˈkæʃ dɪskaʊnt]
to **catch attention**
   [kætʃ əˈtenʃn]
celebrities [səˈlebrətiːz]
chain store [ˈtʃeɪn stɔː]
challenge [ˈtʃælɪndʒ]
charity [ˈtʃærəti]
chart [tʃɑːt]
check-up [ˈtʃekʌp]
client [ˈklaɪənt]

Your translation

co-located, to be ~
   [ˈkəʊləʊˌkeɪtɪd]
to **come as a/no surprise**
   [ˌkʌm əz ə/nəʊ səˈpraɪz]
commercial [kəˈmɜːʃl]
commercial break
   [kəˈmɜːʃl breɪk]
to **commission** [kəˈmɪʃn]
competition [ˌkɒmpəˈtɪʃn]
competitor [kəmˈpetɪtə]
comprehensive
   [ˌkɒmprɪˈhensɪv]
concerned, to be ~
   [kənˈsɜːnd]
to **conduct a survey**
   [kənˌdʌkt ə ˈsɜːveɪ]
confident, to feel ~
   [ˌfiːl ˈkɒnfɪdənt]
consistent [kənˈsɪstənt]
content [ˈkɒntent]
convenience store
   [kənˈviːniəns stɔː]
convenient [kənˈviːniənt]
copywriter [ˈkɒpiraɪtə]
corporate design
   [ˌkɔːpərət dɪˈzaɪn]
corporate identity
   [ˌkɔːpərət aɪˈdentəti]
corporate image
   [ˌkɔːpərət ˈɪmɪdʒ]
to **cover costs** [ˌkʌvə ˈkɒsts]
cross-functional team
   [ˌkrɒsfʌŋkʃənl ˈtiːm]
customer [ˈkʌstəmə]
customer focus
   [ˈkʌstəmə fəʊkəs]
cutting-edge (fashion/
   design) [ˌkʌtɪŋ ˈedʒ]

D
data collection
   [ˌdeɪtə kəˈlekʃn]
data projector
   [ˌdeɪtə prəˈdʒektə]
data volume [ˌdeɪtə ˈvɒljuːm]
decline stage
   [dɪˈklaɪn steɪdʒ]
deep discount
   [diːp ˈdɪskaʊnt]
department [dɪˈpɑːtmənt]
to **devote** [dɪˈvəʊt]
to **dissolve** [dɪˈzɒlv]
to **distinguish sb**
   [dɪˈstɪŋgwɪʃ]
distribution channel
   [ˌdɪstrɪˈbjuːʃn tʃænl]
distributor [dɪˈstrɪbjətə]
to **donate sth** [dəʊˈneɪt]
to **download** [ˈdaʊnləʊd]
to **draw up** [ˌdrɔː ˈʌp]
durable [ˈdjʊərəbl]

Your translation

Your translation

E to **emphasize** ['emfəsaɪz]
employee discount
[ɪm'plɔɪiː dɪskaʊnt]
endorsement [ɪn'dɔːsmənt]
enhanced feature
[ɪn,hɑːnst 'fiːtʃə]
to **establish** [ɪ'stæblɪʃ]
to **evaluate** [ɪ'væljueɪt]
eventful [ɪ'ventfl]
to **examine** [ɪg'zæmɪn]
excerpt ['eksɜːpt]
to **execute** (a marketing
plan) ['eksɪkjuːt]
executive summary
[ɪg,zekjətɪv 'sʌməri]
exhausted, to feel ~
[ɪg'zɔːstɪd]
exhibition [,eksɪ'bɪʃn]
expectation [,ekspek'teɪʃn]
exposure [ɪk'spəʊʒə]
extensive testing
[ɪk,stensɪv 'testɪŋ]
external communication
[ɪk,stɜːnl kəmjuːnɪ'keɪʃn]
eye-catching ['aɪkætʃɪŋ]
eye-inspection
['aɪɪn,spekʃn]

F to **feature** ['fiːtʃə]
fee structure ['fiː strʌktʃə]
to **feel free to do sth**
[,fiːl 'friː]
first double page spread
[fɜːst 'dʌbl peɪdʒ spred]
flat fee ['flæt fiː]
flavour ['fleɪvə]
focus group ['fəʊkəs gruːp]
follow-up phone call
[,fɒləʊ ʌp 'fəʊn kɔːl]
free of charge [friː əv 'tʃɑːdʒ]
free sample [friː 'sɑːmpl]
to **fund** [fʌnd]

G **gatefold** ['geɪtfəʊld]
to **gauge** [geɪdʒ]
to **generate a buzz**
[,dʒenəreɪt ə 'bʌz]
to **get a message across**
[get ə ,mesɪdʒ ə'krɒs]
to **give a speech**
[,gɪv ə 'spiːtʃ]
to **give away** [,gɪv ə'weɪ]
to **go beyond** [,gəʊ bɪ'jɒnd]
to **go out of business**
[gəʊ ,aʊt əv 'bɪznəs]
good value for money
[gʊd ,væljuː fə 'mʌni]
go-to-market strategy
[,gəʊ tə 'mɑːkɪt strætədʒi]
grocery store ['grəʊsəri stɔː]

H **hand-held barcode scanner**
[hændheld 'bɑːkəʊd skænə]
to **handle** ['hændl]
handy ['hændi]
harmful ['hɑːmfl]
health-conscious
['helθ ,kɒnʃəs]
health danger
['helθ deɪndʒə]
horrible ['hɒrəbl]
hype [haɪp]

I **ideally** [aɪ'diːəli]
implementation
[,ɪmplɪmen'teɪʃn]
in advance of [ɪn əd'vɑːns əv]
in charge of, to be ~
[ɪn 'tʃɑːdʒ əv]
in effect, to be ~ [ɪn ɪ'fekt]
in their own field
[ɪn ðeər ,əʊn 'fiːld]
inexpensive [,ɪnɪk'spensɪv]
inquiry [ɪn'kwaɪəri]
insertion [ɪn'sɜːʃn]
inside back cover
[ɪn,saɪd 'bæk kʌvə]
inside front cover
[ɪn,saɪd frʌnt kʌvə]
internal communication
[ɪn,tɜːnl kəmjuːnɪ'keɪʃn]
Internet access
[,ɪntənet 'ækses]
introduction phase
[,ɪntrə'dʌkʃn feɪz]
item ['aɪtəm]

J **job description**
[dʒɒb dɪ'skrɪpʃn]
to **justify** ['dʒʌstɪfaɪ]

K to **keep track** [kiːp 'træk]
to **keep up to date**
[kiːp ,ʌp tə 'deɪt]
key [kiː]
kitchen appliance
['kɪtʃɪn əplaɪəns]

L to **launch a product**
[,lɔːntʃ ə 'prɒdʌkt]
lead [liːd]
leaflet ['liːflət]
to **liaise** [li'eɪz]
light-weight ['laɪtweɪt]
location [ləʊ'keɪʃn]
to **log onto** [,lɒg 'ɒntə]
loss leader ['lɒs liːdə]

M **mail order** [,meɪl 'ɔːdə]
mailing list ['meɪlɪŋ lɪst]
to **maintain a database**
[meɪn,teɪn ə 'deɪtəbeɪs]
to **make a donation**
[,meɪk ə dəʊ'neɪʃn]
to **make a note**
[,meɪk ə 'nəʊt]

	Your translation		Your translation
to **man a stand** [ˌmæn ə 'stænd]		**price war** ['praɪs wɔ:]	
to **market sth** ['mɑ:kɪt]		**proceeds** ['prəʊsi:dz]	
market research [ˌmɑ:kɪt rɪ'sɜ:tʃ]		**product differentiation** [ˌprɒdʌkt dɪfərenʃi'eɪʃn]	
market research company [ˌmɑ:kɪt rɪ'sɜ:tʃ kʌmpəni]		**product life cycle** [ˌprɒdʌkt 'laɪf saɪkl]	
market share [ˌmɑ:kɪt 'ʃeə]		**product line** ['prɒdʌkt laɪn]	
marketing tool ['mɑkɪtɪŋ tu:l]		**product portfolio** [ˌprɒdʌkt pɔ:t'fəʊliəʊ]	
mature [mə'tʃʊə]		**product shot** ['prɒdʌkt ʃɒt]	
media buyer ['mi:diə baɪə]		**profit margin** ['prɒfɪt mɑ:dʒɪn]	
media coverage ['mi:diə kʌvərɪdʒ]		**profitability** [ˌprɒfɪtə'bɪləti]	
media outlet ['mi:diə ˌaʊtlet]		to **promote a brand** [prə,məʊt ə 'brænd]	
medication [ˌmedɪ'keɪʃn]		to **proofread** ['pru:fri:d]	
medium-sized company [ˌmi:diəmsaɪzd 'kʌmpəni]		**proofs** [pru:fs]	
me-too product [ˌmi: 'tu: prɒdʌkt]		**prototype** ['prəʊtətaɪp]	
monetary ['mʌnɪtri]		**proven track record** [pru:vn 'træk rekɔ:d]	
money-back guarantee [mʌni bæk gærən'ti:]		to **provide** [prə'vaɪd]	
mono ['m nəʊ]		**punctuation** [ˌpʌŋktʃu'eɪʃn]	
		purchase ['pɜ:tʃəs]	
N to **negotiate** [nɪ'gəʊʃieɪt]		to **put at the heart of sth** [ˌpʊt ət ðə 'hɑ:t əv]	
neighbourhood store ['neɪbəhʊd stɔ:]		to **put yourself in some-body's shoes** [pʊt jəself ɪn ˌsʌmbədiz 'ʃu:z]	
O **off-brand, to be ~** [ɒf 'brænd]		**Q** **quadrant** ['kwɒdrənt]	
on a positive note [ɒn ə 'pɒzətɪv nəʊt]		**quarter page** ['kwɔ:tə peɪdʒ]	
on behalf of [ɒn bɪ'hɑ:f əv]		**questionnaire** [ˌkwestʃə'neə]	
organigram [ɔ:'gænɪgræm]			
organizer ['ɔ:gənaɪzə]		**R** to **raise** [reɪz]	
out of touch, to be ~ [aʊt əv 'tʌtʃ]		to **rank** [ræŋk]	
outlet store ['aʊtlet stɔ:]		**rate sheet** ['reɪt ʃi:t]	
outline ['aʊtlaɪn]		to **realize** ['rɪəlaɪz]	
to **outsource** ['aʊtsɔ:s]		**recently** ['ri:sntli]	
overheads ['əʊvəhedz]		**reception** [rɪ'sepʃn]	
		to **recognize** ['rekəgnaɪz]	
P to **pass on** [ˌpɑ:s 'ɒn]		**refreshments** [rɪ'freʃmənts]	
to **pay attention** [peɪ ə'tenʃn]		to **reinforce** [ˌri:ɪn'fɔ:s]	
per-capita income [pə 'kæpɪtə ɪnkʌm]		**reliable, to be ~** [rɪ'laɪəbl]	
perception [pə'sepʃn]		**remotely** [rɪ'məʊtli]	
pilot project ['paɪlət,prɒdʒekt]		to **report to sb** [rɪ'pɔ:t tə]	
to **place a press release** [ˌpleɪs ə 'pres rɪli:s]		**reputation** [ˌrepju'teɪʃn]	
pleasantry ['plezntri]		to **require attention** [rɪ,kwaɪə ə'tenʃn]	
pop-up-window ['pɒpʌp wɪndəʊ]		**research process** [rɪ'sɜ:tʃ prəʊses]	
to **pose** [peʊz]		**respondent** [rɪ'spɒndənt]	
PR agency [ˌpi: 'ɑ:r eɪdʒənsi]		**response rate** [rɪ'spɒns reɪt]	
to **pre-program** [ˌpri:'prəʊgræm]		**responsible for, to be ~** [rɪ'spɒnsəbl fə]	
press conference ['pres kɒnfərəns]		**retailer** ['ri:teɪlə]	
press release ['pres rɪli:s]		**retired, to be ~** [rɪ'taɪəd]	
to **prevent** [prɪ'vent]		**revenue** ['revənju:]	
		to **revise** [rɪ'vaɪz]	
		roll-out ['rəʊl aʊt]	
		S **salary** ['sæləri]	
		sales lead ['seɪlz li:d]	
		sales projection ['seɪlz prə,dʒekʃn]	

Your translation

sales records ['seɪlz,rekɔːdz]
sales representative
['seɪlz reprɪzentətɪv]
to schedule a meeting
[,ʃedjuːl ə 'miːtɪŋ]
scientifically proven
[saɪən,tɪfɪkli 'pruːvn]
seamlessly ['siːmləsli]
search engine ['sɜːtʃ endʒɪn]
search term ['sɜːtʃ tɜːm]
to set expectations
['set ekspek'teɪʃnz]
shop assistants
['ʃɒp əsɪstənts]
shopping cart ['ʃɒpɪŋ kaːt]
to simplify ['sɪmplɪfaɪ]
to skyrocket ['skaɪrɒkɪt]
social event [səʊʃl ɪ'vent]
soft drink [,sɒft 'drɪŋk]
to soften criticism
[,sɒfn 'krɪtɪsɪzm]
specifically [spə'sɪfɪkli]
stand, exhibition ~
[,eksɪ'bɪʃn stænd]
to stay ahead of
[,steɪ ə'hed əv]
to stay in touch
[,steɪ ɪn 'tʌtʃ]
sticker ['stɪkə]
street interview
['striːt ɪntəvjuː]
strength [streŋθ]
to supervise ['suːpəvaɪz]
to support [sə'pɔːt]
survey group ['sɜːveɪ gruːp]

T tabulated information
[,tæbjəleɪtɪd ɪnfə'meɪʃn]
to take away [,teɪk ə'weɪ]
to take for a walk
[,teɪk fər ə 'wɔːk]
target ['taːgɪt]
to target ['taːgɪt]
target group ['taːgɪt gruːp]
task [taːsk]
test call ['test kɔːl]
to testify ['testɪfaɪ]
testimonial [,testɪ'məʊniel]
tight budget [taɪt 'bʌdʒɪt]
till [tɪl]
tool [tuːl]
to track [træk]
tracking-system
['trækɪŋ sɪstəm]
trade discount
['treɪd dɪskaʊnt]
trade fair ['treɪd feə]
trade magazine
['treɪd mægəziːn]
trial period [,traɪəl 'pɪəriəd]
trustworthy, to be ~
['trʌstwɜːði]

Your translation

U unique selling point (USP)
[juˌniːk 'selɪŋ pɔɪnt]
user friendly, to be ~
[juːzə 'frendli]

V visible ['vɪzəbl]

W weakness ['wiːknəs]
wealthy ['welθi]
wholesaler ['həʊlseɪlə]
wine tasting [waɪn 'teɪstɪŋ]
worthless ['wɜːθləs]

Y yesterday's news, to be ~
[,jestədeɪz 'njuːz]

Glossary

advertising agency
A company that creates advertisements and plans an advertising campaign. Can also deal with branding and other promotional efforts.

advertising schedule
An advertising schedule shows the topics planned for forthcoming issues of a magazine or newspaper, so that advertisers can choose to advertise in a relevant issue (e.g. a travel agency in an issue dedicated to travel).

art director
The person responsible for the design and production of an advertisement. The art director supervises the design staff.

banner ad
An online advertisement at the top, bottom, or side of a website, containing a link to another website.

benchmarking
Comparing a product, service, or company to others in order to establish a standard.

billboard
A large outdoor advertisement, often appearing alongside roads or in city centres.

blanket family name
A company uses a blanket family name when all its products contain the same name (e.g. Heinz ketchup, baked beans, etc.).

brand equity
The value (either real or perceived) of a brand.

brand loyalty
A strong consumer preference for one brand.

brand values
The values according to which a company makes its decisions related to that brand.

branding
The process of giving a product or service a specific identity, e.g. establishing its brand values and communicating these to the consumer.

break-even point
The point at which the volume of revenues equals the company's total expenses.

bulk discount
A bulk discount is given to customers buying a large amount, e.g. a clothing shop buying 10,000 shirts might receive a bulk discount from a clothing manufacturer.

buzz
The aim of many marketing campaigns is to generate a buzz, i.e. to get people talking about a product.

captive product pricing
Charging a high amount for an item that complements a low-cost item. For example, a razor is often cheap, but razor blades (the captive product) are, comparatively, very expensive.

cash discount
A discount offered for payment in cash.

circulation
The number of readers a publication reaches.

copywriter
The person who writes the text for advertisements.

corporate identity
The identity of a company as formed by its name, logo, slogan, and the language used by the company to describe itself.

demographic information
Information such as age, gender, and income.

direct marketing
Marketing directly to the customer using letters, leaflets, catalogues, door-to-door selling, etc. The term is occasionally also used to include tele-marketing.

distribution channel
The route a company uses to distribute its goods. For example, a manufacturing company's distribution channel might go from factory to wholesaler to retailer.

economy pricing
Pricing items very low to encourage sales. This is the pricing model used for generic products.

field research
Market research done outside the company using observation or surveys with questionnaires.

focus group
A focus group is a small group of people brought together to answer market research questions.

generic
Generic products are products without a brand name.

geographical pricing
Pricing items according to where they are being sold. Items sold in poorer countries, for example, might be priced lower.

giveaway
An item, such as a pen or key chain, that prominently features the company's logo, given away for free to promote that company.

going rate
The average cost of a product or service.

hoarding (BE) → billboard (AE)

hypermarket
A huge store containing all the features of a super-market, department store, and drugstore/chemist's.

to launch
Something is launched when it is introduced onto the market in an attention-getting way, for instance through special events or a high-profile marketing campaign.

market research
The process of learning about what products and services people want and what price they're willing to pay.

market segment
A group of consumers who share a similar buying behaviour.

market share
The percentage of the total market held by a given company. For example, if 20 % of the toothpaste sold in the UK is made by Fresh, then Fresh holds 20 % of the market share.

marketing plan
A detailed plan describing how a product or service will be marketed.

media mention
An item about a company in a newspaper, magazine, online publication, on television, or on the radio.

4 Ps
Product, price, placement, and promotion. These four points must be considered by every marketing professional.

penetration pricing
Pricing something very low to gain market share. Penetration pricing is normally used only for a limited period of time.

placement
Vis-à-vis the 4 Ps, placement refers to the distribution channels through which a product is sold.

premium pricing
Pricing a product or service high in order to establish it as a luxury item.

press release
A short text distributed to journalists giving information on a product, event, or person.

price
The amount of money a product or service costs.

price skimming
The practice of charging a high price for a product or service that only your company offers. Once competitors enter the market, this pricing model is no longer possible.

price war
A competition between companies to offer the lowest prices; a price war involves a series of price cuts.

product endorsement
A positive comment by a satisfied customer (sometimes a celebrity) used to advertise a product.

product life cycle
The typical product life cycle consists of four stages: introduction, growth, maturity, and decline.

product line
A related series of items sold by a company. For example, printers are one of HP's product lines.

product portfolio
All the products sold by a company. Also called 'product mix'.

promotion
Promotion refers to the ways in which potential customers are made aware of your product.

promotional discount
A temporary discount offered on a product to encourage sales.

psychographic information
Information on a consumer's lifestyle, beliefs, and values.

public relations officer
A public relations officer creates and maintains good relations between his or her organization and the public.

rate sheet
A sheet listing the prices for advertising in a magazine, newspaper, or on a website.

rebranding
Creating a new brand identity for a product or service.

recommended retail price
The selling price suggested by the manufacturer.

respondent pool
The people to whom a survey or questionnaire is sent. The people who actually respond are called respondents.

response rate
The percentage of people who respond to a questionnaire or a direct marketing campaign.

retail store
A store where private individuals shop.

slogan
A short, memorable sentence used to advertise a company or product, e.g. Nike: *Just do it*.

target market
The group to which a company intends to sell.

telemarketing
Marketing by means of telephone calls.

user profile
Customer information stored electronically, especially for online shoppers.

USP
A USP, or unique selling proposition, states the unique benefit of buying or using a product.

vehicle ad
An advertisement placed on a bus, train, or automobile.

wholesaler
A company which distributes manufacturers' products to retailers and other distributors. Usually, they do not sell to the end-users directly.

Useful phrases and vocabulary

PARTICIPATING IN DISCUSSIONS

Giving your opinion
I think / feel that …
It would be great to …
We definitely should …

Agreeing
Me too. / Me neither.
Yes, and …
That's true.
Good point.

Disagreeing
I don't think …
That would be (free), which is nice, but …
Sure, but …
I don't know …
I see what you mean, but …

Asking others for their opinion
What do you think, [name]?
[Name], do you agree?
[Name], would you like to say a few words about that?

TALKING ABOUT JOB DESCRIPTIONS

The job involves …
You / The successful candidate will be responsible for …
The right person will be in charge of …
Direct responsibilities include …

PRESENTING YOUR IDEAS

We think / feel that …
In our opinion, the best options are …
The most effective values for our company would be …

SURVEY QUESTIONS

Could I ask you how much you would pay for (the phone)?
How important are the following features to you?
Which other features are important to you?
How interested would you be in buying such a product?
How often would you …?
Can you tell me more about that?
When did you last …?
What would you like / be willing to …?

EMAIL LANGUAGE

Greetings & Closes
Dear Ms Flores – Yours sincerely (very formal)
Hello Geoff – Best wishes (neutral)
Hi Martin – All the best (informal)

Pleasantries
Hope all's well with you.
How was your weekend?

Closes for saying thank you
Many thanks (more formal)
Thanks for your help (informal)
Cheers (informal and British)

TELEPHONING

Hello, [company]. [name] speaking.
Hello, this is [name] from [company]. I'd like to speak to [name].
Just a moment. I'll put you through.
Speaking. What can I do for you?

DISCUSSING AN AD CAMPAIGN

Typically, our products have appealed to … . We'd like to change our image.
Our X are very well known, but we want to raise the profile of our …
We want to appeal to a younger / an older audience.
We want to change perceptions of our product.
We want to reinforce our brand's positive image.
We'd like to rebrand our product.
We have a high market share among teenagers / 18–25-year-old men. We want to create ads that appeal to women in the same age range.
Our ads should appeal to …
It's important for us to create a new image.

WRITING PRESS RELEASES

To start a press release
[Company] announced today that …
[Company] is proud to announce the launch of the new …
[Company] is introducing …

To end a press release
For more information about …, contact …
More information about … can be found at www.company.com.
Businesses interested in more information on … should contact …

GIVING FEEDBACK

Thank you for your draft of [*date*].
We are very happy with ...
We really like ...
We're very happy with what you've done.
We think that the design is too conservative / unconventional / ...
The colours are too bright / dull.
We think that the images might be too ...
We're a little concerned about ...
How about ... instead?
Could you add a picture of ...?
Could you please remember to ...?
We need to add information on ...
It's important to mention that ...
The letter should highlight ... / We'd like to highlight ...
We want to stress ...
One point to emphasize is ...

TRADE FAIR QUESTIONS

Could you tell me more about your company?
Do you offer ...?
Would it be possible to be put on your mailing list?
How can I reach you?
Do you have some information I can take away?
Excuse me, are these pens to take away?
Where are you based?

SOCIALIZING

Hi, I'm ... . – Nice to meet you.
Is this your first trip to [*Britain*]?
Where are you staying?
How are you enjoying the fair so far?
What area of [*biotech*] do you work in?
  – I'm in [*sales*].
I work for a company called [*Natural Solutions*].
Do you have a card? – Here, let me give you my card.

USEFUL VERBS (IN CONTEXT)

to associate	Our aim is to find out exactly what people associate with our logo.
to attract	I hope that the additional services will attract new customers.
to be in effect	The special offer will be in effect for a year to try to increase sales.
to catch attention	I think the colours need to be a bit brighter to catch people's attention.
to come as a/no surprise	The drop in sales came as no surprise after so much bad publicity.
to conduct a survey	We're conducting a survey to see what people think about our service.
to distinguish onself	How can we distinguish ourselves from our competitors?
to establish a brand	Customers seem to like our ideas, we just need to establish our brand.
to feature	OK, but which products should feature in the magazine?
to get your message across	We need more press coverage to get our message across to potential customers.
to go beyond	Our restaurants should go beyond the 'fish & chips' image of British food.
to keep track of	We need to keep track of new companies entering the market.
to market sth	I think we should market the technology in different countries.
to promote a brand	We're going to promote our new catalogue in Spain.
to put at the heart of	We put our commitment to road safety at the heart of our campaign.
to raise	Let's have a meeting with marketing to discuss raising prices.
to rank	Our company ranks highly in terms of research.
to reinforce	We want to reinforce our image as a socially responsible company.
to set expectations	Many young professionals set their expectations very high.
to stay ahead of	Does anyone have any creative new ideas to help us stay ahead of our competitors this year?
to target	I think we need to target our younger readers more.
to track	The software tracks how people move around our website.